Blood of the Sword
Blood of the Cross

A fanatical Muslim tells his story

Reza F. Safa

Sovereign World
STL Books, Bromley

Sovereign World Ltd
P.O. Box 17   Published jointly with
Chichester   STL Books (Send the Light),
PO20 6YB   P.O. Box 48, Bromley, Kent,
England   BR1 3JH, England.

Scripture quotations are taken from the New King James Bible © Thomas Nelson Inc; Nashville, U.S.A.

British Library Cataloguing in Publication Data
Safa, Reza F.
  Blood of the sword, blood of the cross.
  1. Iran Christianity. Conversion to Christianity biographies
  I. Title
  248.246092

  ISBN 1-85240-041-2
  STL ISBN 1-85078-084-6

Typeset by the Ikthos Studios, Andover, Hampshire.

Contents

Acknowledgements

My sincere gratitude to my Lord who allowed me to write this book as a witness to many people.

Also to my wife, Marilyn, who has been a wonderful partner and faithful in serving the Lord together with me. To my pastor, Bror Spetz, whose love and support has been a great encouragement to me. And special thanks to Andy Hutchings and my wife for correcting the English of the manuscript.

Dedicated to my dearest brothers, Lars Berntsson and Borje Eggefors, whose true love and testimony made me see the love of Christ.

Chapter 1

Iran - the Homeland

"Evert," I said through my chattering teeth, "I just have to change my seat." I was freezing. The temperature was -20°C. We were travelling on an old bus, possibly one left over from World War II. The windows were frosted over and there must have been a hole somewhere because in spite of our heavy jackets, hats and gloves, we could still feel a cold wind blowing. A heater on the bus was beyond one's wildest imagination. The breath of the people, packed in like sardines, was the only warmth I could feel.

The natives, obviously more accustomed to this mode of travel than we, were dressed in long, thick sheepskin overalls with furry Russian-style hats. Women had their heads completely swaddled in shawls. They got on and off the bus with their chickens and packages wrapped in handkerchiefs as the bus made stops in different villages along the mountain route. The road was snowy so we travelled no faster than 30 kilometres per hour. It was terribly cold and dark on the bus. There was only one little glimmering light. I had to change my seat. I could feel the draught through to my bones. Evert was shrunken down in his jacket with his head bowed and his chin and mouth inside the collar. "Okay," he said. We didn't talk much during that five-hour bus ride through the mountains.

I found an empty seat at the rear of the bus next to a Romanian woman. My heart was full of love and compassion for these poor, depressed people. I have travelled to 24 different countries around the world and I've never seen anywhere that people are so oppressed and poor as in Romania. I wondered what in the world I was doing here, but my heart was beating love. Oh, how grateful I felt toward the Lord, as I thought back to where I had come from.

I was born in the city of Teheran, the capital of Iran, which means "the land of Arians", biblically known as Persia. Teheran is a large city of about seven million people. Although very polluted, it is a beautiful city lying at the foot of the Alborz mountain range. Teheran is situated in the north-west of Iran, having beautiful green valleys and rivers on the north toward the Caspian sea and dry salt land in the south, and is a unique city with a character all of its own.

I come from a fairly large family. Of nine brothers and sisters I am next to youngest, and my mother's only son. My father had had another wife with whom he had my four half-brothers and sisters before he met my mother. She was fourteen years of age when they married. Being so young and marrying a man twice her age was not easy for her, but this kind of arrangement was very common when she was young.

Mother comes from a large, simple family compared with dad's more complicated background.

My father was pretty much the centre of our home, a man of authority, hard-working and with a quick temper. Mum called him a dictator sometimes. By profession Dad was a cloth merchant experiencing several successes and also bankruptcies in his time. By nature he is a poet, a very gifted man and versed in old Persian poetry.

Poetry is one of the main bases of literature and culture in Persia. Poets like Hafez, Saadi and Khayyam are internationally known. Persian poetry is part of the daily language of the people. Often one will hear someone refer to a poem in order to put an idea across in a normal discussion.

My father is a true admirer of Persian literature. Even after two years of college education I still had a hard time with the old poetry - I don't mean understanding it, just simply reading it correctly! How Dad would sometimes laugh when I tried to read him one of those poems! He who knows the A to Z of poetry! He to whom poetry is life! He who has such a love of poetry and whose commitment to it is unparalleled! One has to live with him in order to understand what I mean. My father's love for poetry made him a poet. To the scholars, he is one of the best authorities on traditional poetry. And though he has been writing for over 50 years since he was a teenager, he never desired to be known or wished to go into print before his death. Only recently has my father changed his mind and published four books in the Persian language.

I know Mother's family fairly well, but except for having contact with two of my aunts I know little about my father's relatives. He did not talk much about them at home. I do know that he had a very hard time in his youth and started to work at a very early age, and for some reason there was a barrier between him and his family which seemed to affect his relationship with us.

I sometimes remember seeing him working hard to support us and provide for our needs and other times when he would stay at home writing poetry. He would sit on the balcony with his pen and a piece of paper in his hand musing. Father was often lost in his own world of deep thoughts while smoking a lot of cigarettes. It seemed that every five minutes my mother would walk out to him with a cup of *chai*.[1] He loved to write, and drink chai. There was a tug-of-war between us and his writing. My mother was not exactly an admirer of poetry nor an encourager of my father's work and, sadly, this became one of the reasons for the many conflicts and quarrels we often faced at home. It was like the poverty of the painter and his need to paint.

There have been different periods in my father's life and two major life-styles. There was the time when he was a party man, drinking alcohol and having *bazm*[2] with his poet friends, and the other when he

1. Tea made on a Samavar.
2. Festivity for the art.

4

was fanatically religious. In my early teenage life I remember seeing many of dad's friends visiting our home. They would get together partying, drinking alcohol, reading poetry and eating constantly until late into the night. We would all work hard to prepare food for all these people. My mother would sweat all day long in the kitchen, making several delicious dishes for the guests. My father was a very rough and temperamental man. In my youthful way, I used to like him best when he was drunk because he would be very gentle and calm with me. As far as I remember, if I ever got any hugs from him, it was when he was drunk. But at the same time he could get nasty and fight with my mother and beat her, and we would all cry and have a miserable time.

My worst memories are from my teenage years. Financially we had it rough. Dad was in a lot of debt for which he spent some time in jail. My older sister had a nervous breakdown. My father's drinking and fighting at home made it very difficult for us and so it was that my heart grew cold towards my father. Seeing him beating my mother and watching her crying helplessly made me hate him. There wasn't any father-son relationship between us. He never called me son, only my name, Reza, and I called him *agha* (sir) and as the days went by I could feel the distance between us growing. I had lost respect for him. There was only a sense of competition and rejection between us. I could do nothing to make him happy and he never made me proud of who I was. There was a lack of love for my father in me and I felt it more strongly as time passed. Sometimes when we got into a quarrel and he cursed or hit me, I wanted to run away from home, but then I would think of my mother. Somehow I was more like her boy than his. Whenever that feeling of rejection and loneliness came over me I would take a bus to my eldest sister's home. She and her family meant a lot to me. They gave me the respect and love that I missed at home. In our culture we are taught to respect our elders, especially our parents. So whenever my dad got into a fight with me I just kept my mouth shut and my head bowed and walked away crying and talking to God, who I was not sure of — nor if He heard me.

In my late teenage life there was a drastic change in my father's behaviour. He stopped partying and drinking and became very religious. There had been several occasions in his life when he swayed back and forth between a worldly life and Islam. My family usually didn't believe he would stick to it, but this time it was very serious. As they would say in Persian, he had poured the water of repentance over his head. Father became a fanatical Muslim. To a fanatical Muslim, Islam is not only a religion but a life-style. It is a system in which political, social, economic and religious elements are combined.

There are two major divisions among Muslims; the Shi'ite's[3] and the Sunni's.[4] 91 percent of the

3. Followers of Ali as Mohammed's successor.
4. Followers of Omar as Mohammed's successor.

population of Iran are Shi'ite. Among the different divisions, they are the most militant and fanatical concerning the *shariat*.[5] This is one of the reasons why such a drastic change took place in the country after the fall of the Shah.

My father was a very knowledgeable man concerning the *shariat*. He knew Arabic and was well acquainted with the Qur'an.[6] He kept his Namaz[7] and sometimes even *namaz shab*.[8] Father was an admirer of Ali[9] as the greatest hero of Islam after Mohammed, and had an unshakeable love in his heart for the imams (pontiffs) of Islam. However, there is no such thing as close contact or fellowship with God. God is too great a being to be contacted by man. Therefore the prophet and imams are the closest beings that man can approach and they are accounted so holy that there is awesome respect for them. Because the Shi'ite Muslims believe that these imams are very close to God, to express one's love toward them is to express one's love toward God, and this is the reason why my father wrote so much in veneration of Ali.

Becoming religious, however, and a fanatic, did not affect my father's temperament and character. Although the outward had been changed, the inside was still the same - the same old 'Dad'.

5. The Islamic law.

6. Islam's holy book.

7. Stipulated prayers in Arabic (obligatory) offered five times daily.

8 Extra stipulated prayers (voluntary).

9. Shi'ite Islam, Mohammed's successor.

As far as I remember I always believed in the existence of God. I started to practise being a faithful Muslim in my early years. I kept the laws and regulations. I prayed five times a day, and fasted during the whole month of Ramadan.[10] There was a love in my heart for God which, I believe, I received from my father, who although being a hard man, had a strong love and tenderness towards God. I remember sometimes waking up in the middle of the night and seeing him reading his Qur'an and crying. I never saw him cry except when he was praying to God alone. He was very proud of me when I kept all the thirty days of the fast, which not many young people used to manage at that time.

According to the law, a person who fasts is not allowed to eat or drink as long as it is daylight. My younger sister and I were the two in the family who fasted the most. My mother and father were exempted because their bodies weren't strong enough to bear it. We ate twice each day during the fasting month, once before sunrise, and again after sunset. Mother would get up early, about two hours before dawn, to prepare a meal and drinks for us. I would eat, and especially drink, as much as I could before my morning prayers – and then go back to sleep. If Ramadan happened to fall during summertime, fasting would be very difficult because of the intense heat as well as the long days. Sometimes my body would become so dehydrated that I would feel weak to the point of

10. The ninth month of the Islamic lunar year.

8

fainting. There are people who damage their body in this way. I also knew of people who took a mouthful of water in secret — but I refused to give up. I wanted to please God with all my strength, so I would sometimes take a hose in the yard and pour water over my heated body. Late in the afternoon, mother would prepare a delicious Persian dish with some soup and salad, and make everything ready for the time of *eftar*.[11] As soon as the *azan*[12] was heard on the TV, I would attack the food like a hungry lion. Oh my, it felt so good.

There is another religious month for the Shi'ite Muslim which is also held sacred. It is called Moharram.[13] Moharram is the month of mourning in remembrance of the martyrdom of the imams. During Moharram people dress in dark colours and hold feasts of mourning. Some have *rhozeh*[14] in their homes. My family and relatives were very active during Moharram. My aunt gave Nazr[15] and would give a *ghorbany*[16] and my mother was usually the cook. Together with my uncle they would make a fire in the back yard and cook kilos of rice and stew in cauldrons which we would all help to distribute in the neighbourhood. As a young lad I used to search for the neighbourhood where kebab was being served.

11. End of fast days.
12. Call to prayer.
13. The first month of the Islamic lunar year.
14. Gathering for the recital of the tragedies of martyrs.
15. Make a vow.
16. An offering of food given to the poor.

That was my favourite food!

During Moharram it is not uncommon for religious people to hire a *mullah*[17] for a few hours. Relatives and neighbours come and listen to the stories of martyrdom of the imams narrated by the mullah while all the people cry and beat their chests. I would sometimes join the *rhozeh* but I never really liked that crying business. To me it was an act of hypocrisy because some of the mourners didn't go regularly to *namaz*.

During Moharram I would join the local group of young people at nights and go for *sinehzani*.[18] We would march through the streets and alleys of each neighbourhood carrying flags stained with the blood of the sacrificed lamb. Holding *zanjir*,[19] we would beat our heads and shoulders chanting the hymns of sorrows for the dead imams. Another group of daring young people would also march through the streets mourning. However, there was a difference. They were fanatical and violent. Using *zanjir*, we would beat ourselves to show our grief but these people used *qameh*.[20] Dressed in white and with shaven heads, they marched through the streets singing mourning hymns and hit their heads open with a sword. The bloodshed made an awful sight and it was not unknown for some of them to become infected in their brain and die.

17. Muslim priest.
18. March of mourning
19. A lash with short chains.
20. A short straight sword.

Sometimes I made a pilgrimage together with my family to the city of Meshhed where the shrine of the eighth imam of Islam lies. There, I would personally offer my most important prayers, make a vow, and pray constantly towards Mecca.

However, keeping all th*e shariat* was not an easy task. The *namaz* and fasting, the mourning, the so many regulations of washing and cleansing, the food restrictions and so on were a heavy burden. How I wanted to keep them all! Oh how I wanted to please God!

But keeping all the laws and commandments of Islam and trying to do good was not enough. I could still feel a lack of peace and joy in my heart. There was something missing in my life! Though relatives and friends always admired me as "the man who is perfect in the law and doing righteousness before God", deep inside I knew I was not close to Him.

Not coming from a rich family made me think that the answer to my emptiness might lie in money and a highly respected social position. Iran was on the verge of developing into a modern society. Higher education was the goal of many a young person. Mother wanted me to be a doctor. Of course, that was the dream of all mothers. Father wanted me to take over his business and become wealthy. I myself wanted both. I always dreamed of making them proud of me, and having enough money to support them in their retirement. The private sector of society in Iran does not provide social security or pensions. It is the children who take responsibility for their parent's old age.

With 1978 came the beginning of political unrest in the country. It wasn't long before we heard shouting from demonstrations in the streets of Teheran, and in our own neighbourhood: "Down with the Shah," "Khomeini is our imam." It was then that I heard of Ayatollah[21] Khomeini for the first time in my life. Shootings and screaming and bloodshed were shaking the foundation of the Shah's regime. Khomeini became more and more popular as he dispatched his preaching tapes against the Shah from his temporary home in Paris where he was in exile. People reckoned on him as their future leader and as the only one who could pull down the mighty government and army. They would be set free from the Shah's oppressive reign. To myself and many fanatical muslims, Khomeini was an imam, not in the rank of "the Twelve" but nevertheless the closest person to God on the face of the earth, and we revered him as our leader and hero.

In the summer of 1978 I graduated from high school and was forced to help my father in his business. The conflict between us increased all the more. I was also unable to pass the university entrance examination, making further studies in Teheran an impossibility. Somehow though, there arose an urge within me to leave the country in order

21. High priest.

to continue them abroad. I knew that my family would not be able to support me for further education so I had to find a place where I could study and work at the same time. After gathering information, I made the decision to apply to a college in Texas, USA. My family did not take me seriously when I told them of the chances of my leaving for the USA. But when news of my acceptance by the college arrived it shocked them all.

Chapter 2

Trip to the West

The big day finally arrived. The time had come to leave my homeland and my family. Everyone came to the airport to see me off. There were so many of them: my brothers and their families, my sisters and their families, and friends. A big crowd with sad faces. My mother was the saddest of all. She cried a lot and expressed her love continuously. I was the apple of her eye. I was, after all, her only son.

I myself was experiencing a mixture of feelings. A part of me was already missing the fellowship, the friendship, the fights, the laughter, the noise and the crowd of this great and different family of mine.

Family ties are very strong in Iran. Eight brothers and sisters, their spouses, and uncountable numbers of children kept our lives very busy. We were always in and out of each other's homes. Visits were kept short during the week but on Fridays[1] we were either invited to someone's home or we had guests over. Sometimes everyone came to our home since "Father's home" is the centre of all activity. It was chaotic. With all my nieces and nephews it was like

1. Last day of the Muslim week.

a zoo. Dad would often yell at them or pinch their ears to keep them quiet. Nevertheless, we had a great time. We played, joked, laughed, drank a lot of *chai* and ate lots of food and fruits or Persian *ajil*.[2] Conversation usually centred around the people who weren't present, a very common occurrence in Iran. Or we would talk about Dad's ideas of how to make a successful business. We never talked about politics or weather or anything like that. Life centred around our own family and relatives. After all, there were so many of us that we could make a little town or tribe ourselves! It wasn't hard to be closely bound to a family like ours. And being the youngest brother I received extra attention and love from the rest of my brothers and sisters. I was always surrounded by them and it was no easy thing to leave them all and go to a foreign country, to be completely alone and a stranger.

Yet despite the heartbreak of leaving my family, there was a sense of excitement within me. To go to another part of the world and learn new things was very exciting, and I was sure that being free from my father's yoke would be a great release. I wanted to stand on my own feet and prove to him that I could make something out of my life.

After a time at the airport together with my family, the moment had come to say goodbye to them and board the plane. Hugs and kisses were exchanged all round. Many tears were shed.

2. Nuts or seeds seasoned with vinegar.

There were many Americans on the plane leaving Iran and going home. At that time there were one hundred thousand Americans living in Teheran alone. Iran's strategic geographical location was an ace card for the game that America wanted to play with Russia. However, there was fear that the Shah's regime was about to fall and many Americans were leaving Iran. There was much unrest and there were many anti-American demonstrations.

The plane seat next to me was occupied by an American. This was my first contact with a person from another country! I immediately started to practise my English. It was exciting and challenging to move to America. Most of what I knew about the United States I had learned from Hollywood movies.

My dreams were coming true. I'd always liked foreign languages and cultures. In school, English had always been my best subject. Somehow I had a feeling that one day I would travel and work in other countries. I even thought I would marry a foreigner. My sisters used to say that they would love to have a Japanese sister-in-law! I still don't know why.

The plane landed in London to refuel. In the transit area we were given a voucher for refreshments. As I handed mine in at the bar to get a soft drink, the lady behind the counter asked me something which I did not understand. Too proud to ask her to repeat the question, I responded with a "yes". The woman laughed, whispered something to the other waitress, and handed me ten glasses of soft drinks. I

17

realized then that I would have to learn to speak the language properly!

The next stop was New York and my first experience of culture-shock. The plane landed at Kennedy Airport and I had to catch a connecting flight from another terminal to Houston, Texas. There were so many people of so many different colours and backgrounds. Everything seemed double in size - people, cars, buildings. America was a hotchpotch of all the different kinds of people on the earth.

After passing through Immigration, I shared a taxi with an Iranian family who were also going to Houston. The taxi driver charged us six times more than the meter read. I refused to pay and asked for a policeman. But the Iranian family were nervous and rich. They didn't want to argue and so they paid the extra fare. As I walked away from the taxi I remembered the words of my mother, "Son, be careful, they carry guns in Texas." In her simplicity she had thought America would be like the old Western movies. There was some truth in what she said. I had had a taste of that even without a gunman.

We arrived in Houston at 3 am. The Iranian family with whom I'd shared the taxi gave me a ride to a motel where I spent the first night.

The following day I registered at the language school and looked for a room to rent. On asking around, I met an Iranian Muslim who offered me his help and told me that I could room with his group.

I was so grateful to God to meet with that kind man. It helped me overcome the fear of being totally lost and a stranger.

Six of us lived in a house called "the house of Islam", so called because it was an open house for Muslims coming from other states. We often had visitors there from everywhere. Somehow I felt at home there. At least I was surrounded by my own countrymen, people who were also Muslim. But they were very much involved in politics. From the day of my arrival, they started condemning me because I had left Iran and hadn't stayed to fight the Shah. I wondered to myself, "If they are so hot about fighting, why don't they go back and fight themselves?" However, I was very grateful to them. They gave me a place to stay, showed me around, and even found a job for me.

I was not very active in politics. It was a strange game to me and I didn't want to play it. I did, however, follow the news about Khomeini. The situation in Iran was getting worse daily. Many were killed in demonstrations against the government. The casualties were many and each new victim made the fall of the Shah even more certain.

My days were full. During the day I studied. In the evenings I worked as a waiter's assistant, a waiter and a valet parkman. I was happy to be able to support myself without the help of my family.

After seven months of language study in Houston I moved to New Orleans and enrolled in college.

Again, during the days I studied and in the evenings I worked.

Life was different in America. The way of thinking was much different from what I was used to. Time had more value and had an effect on people's relationships which was foreign to me. Materialism and money had more value than people. I was fired sometimes because of that. It was hard to mix friendship with business. I was worth only as much as the profit I could produce.

A year went by and I started to miss my home, my family and friends in Iran. Even though I had found new friends I often felt lonely. One of the reasons for this was my strong belief in Islam and being faithful in practising it. Not drinking alcohol and not smoking marijuana singled me out among these new American friends.

Being counted as religious and narrow-minded, and sometimes even being ridiculed did not stop me from practising the laws of Islam. I continued to do my five times of prayer, and fasted during the month of Ramadan. The majority of Iranian youths were very strongly influenced by the life-style of young Americans. Once they used to pray but now they were smoking marijuana and drinking. I wanted to be a faithful Muslim.

I admit there were times when I was tempted to give up. Fasting was especially hard when I worked as a cook at a pizza restaurant. It was not easy to be forbidden to drink and eat while standing and making pizza in front of a furnace-like oven on the long summer days of New Orleans. But I succeeded. Impatiently I would wait for the sun to go down. I would make a pizza, put it in the oven and look at the sun, make a pizza, put it in the oven, check the sun. Finally, at sunset, I would make myself a huge pizza, pour a huge pitcher of soft drink and break my fast.

In 1979 the Islamic revolution took place in Iran. The Shah fled the country, the government fell, and Ayatollah Khomeini returned to Iran from his many years in exile. He was highly respected by the people as their new leader and imam. To Muslims he was a mighty man who had caused the downfall of the Shah's powerful regime. Much blood had been shed, but people were dreaming of a new and free Iran.

On November 4th of the same year, a group of Muslim students seized the American embassy in Teheran and took the American diplomats hostage. This event caused a definite change of relations between the two countries. This in turn affected the attitude of American people towards the Iranian students living in the United States.

"We should go bomb Iran" was a phrase I often heard from people. People ridiculed Khomeini. They made up funny songs about him. His picture became a dart board and many hated him. I often got into arguments and sometimes even into fights because of these attitudes.

I could not stand the attitude of people in the

United States toward us Iranians. Some people treated us as though we were the ones who had taken the American hostages. I couldn't understand why we were blamed for that. I couldn't understand their attitude of "Let's bomb them" and "We are the best". Sometimes I was reluctant to tell people where I was from. I was afraid someone would take revenge on me.

The fear turned into hatred and I wanted to go back home. I remember one night I was invited to a party. Once people realized I was from Iran the arguments started and I became the object of their ridicule. The only person among them who took my side was a guy the others called a nurd. I left the party, together with that nurd, and I decided to go back to Iran. I decided to fight for Khomeini.

Once again, I was running from rejection.

Chapter 3

The Revolution

I was full of joy and expectation as our plane landed at Mehrabad airport. Although it had been good to be away from my family, I had missed them a lot. Being on my own the past year-and-a-half had taught me a few lessons about life. I wanted to give my family, especially my father, another chance.

Since the revolution, I had heard many good things about the new Iran, how the whole country and the people were affected. I had heard how people were good to one another and that they helped each other with joy. I wanted to be part of it. I wanted to live in a land where the weak weren't pushed, where there was freedom for all people and where there wouldn't be any place for the wicked ones. Oh what a dream! I couldn't wait to see it with my own eyes.

The air felt so good and free as I stepped down from the plane. I didn't even notice the pollution. It smelled like home.

All dressed up in a three-piece shiny suit, I was excited to see my family again. To hug them, to kiss them, and to recognise the smell of home again. I couldn't wait to go through Immigration. There were many people on the other side waving. I strained to see my family. I had let them know of the arrival time. Where were they? I walked through Customs and out into the waiting crowd. But my crowd wasn't there. I waited half an hour before they came, disappointment growing with each passing minute. But then, there they were and all the excitement came rushing back to me. It was indeed good to see them again. We went home and talked until late into the night.

It didn't take long, though, before I noticed that a big change had taken place. It was my second experience of culture-shock. The change was a dramatic one. People's attitude and behaviour were so obviously different. They weren't the same people whom I'd known. With few exceptions, almost everyone I knew had taken on a new personality and a new identity. Even the way people talked was different.

The stark reality of this change was brought home to me the day after my arrival. My brother-in-law drove me to the airport to pick up my luggage which had been lost on the previous day. We waited in line at the claim office for hours. As soon as it was our turn they wanted to close the office. We began to argue with the Customs officer. My brother-in-law got angry with the man and called him a counter-revolutionary. The man became furious and called the guards to throw us out of the building. Not wishing to cause trouble, I asked my brother-in-law not to bother with the man and suggested we leave. Some of the other people who were waiting tried to help and accompanied my brother-in-law out of the hall. As he was leaving, the Customs officer jumped over the counter and ran toward him. He jumped on him and punched him in the mouth. I ran to the officer and tried to reason with him, but he hit me too. I became so mad with him that I too lost control and started to fight. I hit him so hard that his eye immediately turned blue. The police came and wanted to arrest us. Fortunately we settled things and no charges were made against us. I thought to myself, "What a welcome party!"

It seemed as though everyone was disgusted with everyone else. Politics had become the main issue of daily life. Political discussions were heard everywhere. Many different political groups had been established. Almost everyone had a different idea on how to run the country. There were so many different isms and so many ideas that it was confusing. There were young people in every corner of the University of Teheran, inside and outside, selling their newspapers and books and arguing with one another. There were right and left wingers, Marxists and Leninists, Maoists and Capitalists, moderate Muslims and Orthodox Muslims. You could find every ism that exists. Everyone believed in a different political line, as they called it.

I heard people talking about political lines in taxis, at the market places, in the streets, everywhere. It had gone to such an extent that some people even made jokes about it. Once, while riding in a taxi, I saw the driver pull down his window and yell at a driver who had cut into his line of traffic. "What's your line?" he cried out, meaning, "What is your political line on driving?"

The different political ideas had caused a division among my good friends. Once we had been ready to give our lives for one another. Their friendship had now turned into political arguments and hating of one another. What a change!

The Orthodox Muslims had become bold and fanatical and the educated and intellectual people had become Communists. There was constant friction and fighting between these two groups. I was shocked to see this one day when my friend drove me past the University of Teheran. There were crowds of young people gathered in two major groups confronting each other. The university students were holding hands inside the university gates. Outside university, numerous fanatical Muslims were holding sticks, chains and knives ready to fight with the students. I could not believe it. What in the world had happened to these people? Where had this hatred come from? Why were they so bloodthirsty? What had happened to these people who once were known for their hospitality, these people who had given their lives for one another? Hadn't enough blood been shed for the revolution? Was this the freedom for which they had fought? What was going to happen? I asked my friend to drive off as fast as he could. I could smell blood and hate. This was truly not what I had expected to see.

My family, of course, weren't exempt from change either. There was a division between my sisters. One of them had been through a divorce and there was constant tension among them.

I was confused. I had no joy or peace and I didn't know what the answer was any more. My hopes of a dreamland had turned out to be a nightmare. I felt a great emptiness deep inside of me. Somehow I had this feeling that I wasn't in the right place. I had an urge to leave the country again. But to where? Was there any place where I could find peace and meaning for my life?

My mother knew of my unrest. She was a good friend and knew me well. Mother wanted to help me in her own way. She wanted me to get settled and stay in Iran. "The time has come for you to make your own family," she told me one day as we were out shopping together. She even had her suggestion. It was a girl in the family.

Marrying a girl from within the extended family is common in Persian culture. When one marries, he marries not only the girl, but her family as well. It is customary to choose a girl from a good family, a family with name and integrity. That is very important for a Persian man because a girl is influenced by her family. Since one already knows his own family, marrying within the family is safest.

Marriage and its customs are more complicated in Eastern cultures than in the West, and even more so in Iran. The traditions and the ceremonial process of marriage in Iran are unique and unforgettable.

As in the West, it all starts when the couple fall in love. In the olden days, however, many unions were started without any romance, since marriages were arranged by the families.

Today it begins with the couple dating in secret. If they fall in love and everything works out they decide to get married. Then the man must convince his parents that he has found his future wife. His parents then gather information about the girl and her family. This is very common since they have to know of the girl's background. If the information is approved by the boy's parents, they then go to visit the girl and her family.

Usually the girl's parents are more excited about the matter than the boy's parents. This is simply because a teenage girl is a big responsibility for them, and they look forward to passing that responsibility on to the husband. One of the responsibilities is financial because the girl is usually supported by her parents before marriage. They also want their daughter to remain a virgin until she gets married. The loss of virginity is a loss to the name and integrity of the family. A girl who loses her virginity lessens her chances of finding a husband.

The prospective bride does her best to get the approval of the boy's parents on the day of their visit. She puts on the best show of her life. She cooks the best food she has learned to make and serves them with constant care. She knows his parents can make the difference. Certain parents can even checkmate the whole game. Of course, the girl's parents also gather information about a boy's education, work and family.

When the parents of the two families have approved of one another, they make an arrangement for a day of *khostegary*.[1] This day is the beginning of a big celebration. The boy and his immediate family get all dressed up and go to the girl's house. They take some *shirini*[2] and some gifts with them. The future bride and her family prepare themselves for the negotiations and a day of feasting. They serve fruits, tea and food. The marriage arrangements are discussed mostly by the parents of the future couple. They discuss *mehrieh*,[3] *jahazieh*[4] and the wedding feast.

It is not easy to get married in Iran. There are a lot of traditional ceremonies to be kept before the wedding. The main thing to be discussed is *mehrieh*. *Mehrieh* is an amount which the bridegroom agrees to pay to the bride in case the marriage should end in a divorce initiated by him. Of course, a higher amount lowers the risk of the man divorcing any woman. The reasoning behind this tradition is that it will help a divorced woman since it will be more difficult for her to find a job than for a man. There

1. The asking of a hand in marriage.
2. Persian pastry.
3. See explanation in text.
4. Dowry.

is no social help provided for the unemployed in Iran.

Once the parents of the new couple have agreed on *mehrieh* then the matter is almost settled. After this day of *khostegary* a day will be arranged for an engagement party. This party is usually arranged by the girl's parents.

The bridegroom is to buy the rings and jewellery which are offered to the bride at the engagement party. It is a great and exciting day. Many relatives and friends are invited to share their beginning. People eat fruit and food and drink a lot of tea and discuss the wedding and its preparations. The wedding itself is paid for by the bridegroom, whereas the *jahazieh* is paid for by the girl's parents. *Jahazieh* is another tradition which is appreciated best by the bridegroom. It is the furniture and the first necessities of the couple's new home. There are no set rules on how many things the parents of the bride should buy for them. It differs from family to family, depending on their social status and life-style. The richer the girl one marries, the more will be received. It includes things like carpets, a refrigerator, an oven and dishes.

By the time the poor bridegroom is through with the wedding he has spent all his savings and is literally broke. Therefore a good *jahazieh* is gladly accepted by him. The *jahazieh* is carried to the house of the new couple a few days before the wedding.

The days before the wedding are a busy time for both families. The bride's parents are busy shopping for the *jahazieh* and arranging and decorating the apartment. The groom is arranging the hall, the music band, the entertainment and the food.

The day itself starts with the wedding ceremony which is performed by a mullah, usually at one of the homes. That evening a big party is arranged in a rented hall. It is a night full of music, dancing, eating and entertainment.

Thinking about this detailed process of getting married, the work involved and most of all the money needed, scared me. I simply wasn't ready for that kind of commitment. However, to actually be married sounded exciting.

My mother's suggestion of a girl was very tempting. She had picked a fine girl who was not easy to resist. She was my aunt's granddaughter on my father's side, very fine, able, gentle and beautiful.

As a young teenager I had been very fond of her. I remember when they used to come over to our house to visit. I was always nervous about seeing her. I would not talk to her very much. My pride would not let me show my interest in her. Then one day I dared to ask her out. To my surprise she accepted and I discovered that she was more interested in me than I was in her. We went to a movie and had some sandwiches and icecream afterwards. It was my first and last date with her. Somehow I lost interest in her.

But I thought marriage could help my situation, my confusion and fill the emptiness. Having a family of my own would stop my searching. It would keep me busy supporting them instead. Having responsibility would give me something to fight for in life, keeping me occupied, with no time to sit and daydream.

I wasn't in love with her any more or at least did not have the same kind of feelings for her I'd had as a teenager. But I liked her and her way of being. She had what I call "class". She and her family were more interested in the potential marriage than I was, not to mention that my mother and all of my sisters were very fond of her. They were all hoping that I would agree to a union in marriage with her.

Sensing that I wasn't in complete opposition to the matter, my mother and sister, together with her mother, arranged a family trip to Messhed. Of course they took me along!

Their idea worked and their hook got a bite. I agreed to go with my family for the khostegary. The girl and I became engaged and I agreed to a mehrieh of half a million *toman*.[5] We agreed to be engaged and delay marrying until I could finish my university education. It meant waiting a couple of years. I got a job at my brother's merchant company as an interpreter and spent most of my free time with my fiancé and her family.

Well, my folks were happy about the arrangement but I sure wasn't. My feelings inside remained the same. Getting engaged had not filled the great empty void inside. I didn't want to give up my dreams of life like the rest of my brothers and sisters. Some of

5. One Toman is approximately equal to 1/7th of a dollar.

them were satisfied being married and having a family. The others didn't know what to do. They were just existing. I did not want to only exist. I wanted to live. I wanted to achieve something in life, to know the purpose of my being, the meaning and the goal.

The urge came over me to leave the country again. But where could I go? I had three more years left on my student visa for America but the hostage situation hadn't changed. The relations between the two countries weren't any better. President Carter had deported some Iranians and he wasn't too keen on letting others in. I knew I wouldn't be welcome there. That was for sure!

Exploring different possibilities I discovered that the brother of a friend of mine was living in Sweden. So, out of all of Europe I decided to go to Sweden and stay there until the hostage situation was resolved. Then I could go back to America to finish my studies.

I was so restless and the situation in Iran did not make it any better. I had to get away. New surroundings and a new adventure would keep my mind and my heart too busy to be aware of the emptiness.

Once more the news of my leaving brought a lot of tears to the eyes of my loved ones. This time I had to comfort my fiancé as well. She arranged a goodbye party at her home. My brothers and sisters and a lot of friends were invited.

I was not honest and fair with my fiancé about my feelings towards her. Receiving so little love and attention from me after I left the country she called the engagement off.

My family seeing me off at the airport made me very sad. I knew it would be a long time before I would see them again. I didn't know what was wrong. I had made a decision not to return home no matter what would happen to me.

Chapter 4

Jesus, not a Prophet but the Son

On the plane to Sweden I met an Iranian student who told me more about life in Scandinavia. I had no idea what I was doing. My life was like a broken ship tossed by the wind in all different directions and now heading towards the North Sea. I was hoping and waiting for something good to happen to me. I wasn't an adventurer per se but I was looking for something. Why wasn't I satisfied and content like the rest of my family? I could have got married and taken a job in Iran and stayed near my family. What was in me that was dragging me around like a thirsty creature searching after water? What was missing? Was I going to make something out of my life? I wondered if my dad was right about me after all.

With these thoughts swirling in my head the plane landed at Copenhagen airport in Denmark. I took a bus to the central railway station and caught the train for Sweden. In Stockholm, Sweden's capital, I changed trains to Uppsala, a city 70 kilometres further north.

My friend's brother was surprised at my arrival. He hadn't heard that I was coming. However, he let me live with him until I found a place of my own. I was later able to rent a room in a student apartment complex.

The people of Sweden and their culture and language were new to me and seemed strange, yet I found them very peaceful. I seldom saw them fighting or arguing with one another. The climate was very different than that of my home country. Winters are so cold and dark and long. Yet during the few months of summer it is, I believe, the most beautiful place on earth.

The Swedish way of life gave me another culture-shock. Their morals, attitudes and relationships couldn't be more different from those I grew up with. People often live together without getting married. I could not believe my eyes when I saw half-naked people sunbathing not only on beaches, but even in their home neighbourhoods. I often felt out of place talking to people about God when they simply did not even believe in His existence. They would not even bother discussing Him and had a very different attitude toward religion in general. The many government social services had made people very independent of one another. It was such a contrast to how I had been raised. In Iran if someone was unemployed and in need, relatives and close family would get together and help him out. But in Sweden, the social services take care of their needs. Therefore people are more dependent on government help than on their family and not at all upon God. This was very new for me.

My new Iranian friends were not much into politics or religion. They just wanted to have fun. There were other Iranian students in Sweden, however, very active in politics and who were constantly criticizing Khomeini and his government.

As usual, I argued a lot with these Iranian communists. I hated them with a passion. To me they were like robots fed on the theories of Lenin, Mao and Marx. They never spoke normal language. One had to have a lot of knowledge to understand them. To me, they were unclean, and I didn't even want to touch them. After a while, however, I tired of arguing with them.

One day I was invited to a party on the rooftop of a student complex. There were some American exchange students there. Since I knew more English than Swedish I started talking to them. Among them was a girl who wasn't drinking wine like the rest of them. "Why don't you drink wine?" I asked her out of curiosity. I wasn't drinking myself because of the law of Islam. "I am a Christian," she answered. Her reply surprised me. I thought all people in the West were Christians. And in Iran it is the Armenian Christians who own the liquor stores! I knew nothing about Christianity except the things I had learned in the Qur'an and in the teachings of Islam.

The American girl explained her faith in Christ and what the Bible said about Jesus. Talking to her raised a lot of questions in me. I argued and resisted her ideas about Jesus. She told me that she believed "Jesus is the Son of God". That was blasphemy! I had learned through the Qur'an that God is not a man. He has no beginning and no end. The Qur'an says that God is not born and does not give birth. How could God have a son? Who was His wife? To me that girl's belief was very naive and unclean.

I had learned a great respect for Jesus in Islam, but only as a prophet who came before Mohammed. A Muslim believes in the five prophets, each of whom, they believe, had a book - Adam, Noah, Moses, Jesus and Mohammed. Mohammed was the last prophet and had the complete revelation of God.

I told the girl that I believed according to what the Qur'an says, that Jesus was born of the virgin Mary, that Jesus was a prophet before Mohammed, and that Jesus wasn't crucified like the Christians believe. She told me things in the Bible which contradicted my Qur'an. I told her that I believed the Bible was not written by Jesus Himself. His disciples wrote it and we Muslims believe that it has been changed through the years by different people.

I came down very hard on that poor girl, and we argued through the evening at the party. She told me about the Bible and Jesus and I told her about the Qur'an and Mohammed. It seemed like we never came to any end or conclusion in our discussion. I was interested, however, in continuing the argument. The girl seemed to be naive and unintellectual, a very simple person. Yet she was different from the rest of her group. She didn't go out on dates and she did not drink and she didn't use foul language like the others. There was a purity in her that attracted me very much. I wanted to know more about Christianity.

I decided one day to go to the old cathedral in town to talk with the priest. I met a young man there dressed in a black robe, a very gentle looking man. I called him "Father". I had learned that from the movies. I spoke to him in English since I didn't know any Swedish yet. I told him I would be willing to sweep the floor of the cathedral in exchange for learning more about Christianity. He wasn't too keen on the idea of my cleaning but he did introduce me to a friend of his, an American. The American told me about a couple of Swedish guys by the name of Lars and Borje. I phoned them and invited them to come for a visit.

"What strange looking priests," I thought to myself. Standing before me as I opened the door were two tall and skinny men, just the opposite of my stereotype image of priests. They looked very happy and were very friendly, both unusual for Swedes. One of them had a red beard and they were very simply dressed in jeans. "Welcome, fathers," I said as we shook hands. They smiled, "You do not need to call us 'father'," they replied. I later learned that they were not priests, neither were they Catholic. They just had a love for foreigners and wanted to tell them the story of Jesus.

Lars and Borje were very friendly and warm. During the several months that I had resided in Sweden, I had not met any Swede so friendly and happy. Lars, with the red beard, played a guitar and they sang about Jesus. We drank tea and talked a lot. I had a million questions and for each one they turned to their Bibles to find the answer. They seemed to care and they listened.

One day, Lars and Borje invited me to their home. They were neighbours and worked in the same church. I accepted their invitation and visited them. They seemed to be very simple people, not caught up in materialism. I was impressed by their love and care. They had a special joy and peace. They had a light in their eyes that I had not seen in anyone else. It was a pure and genuine light. They spoke mostly about God and Jesus. They did not talk behind people's backs and they did not use any foul language. They were genuinely interested in knowing more about me. I felt at home for the first time in my life.

In the beginning, these people had seemed more naive and weaker than the other Swedes I knew. But the more I got to know them, the more I saw a difference between them and ordinary people. They also invited me to their church and Bible study groups. Our friendship grew and I visited them often.

Everything these Christians did was different from my religion and its teachings. They read the Bible in their own language whereas I had to learn Arabic in order to read the Quran. They prayed simply in their mother tongue whereas I prayed the same words in Arabic five times a day, 365 days a year. They studied and read the Bible more often than I (or any Muslim that I knew) had ever read the Qur'an. They often prayed for one another. They gave generously to the needs of others without expecting it back. I saw no hate or bitterness in them. I never heard them talk negatively about anyone. They did not lie, not even "little white lies". They were willing to forgive if asked. Their friendship wasn't based on getting some- thing from someone, but was pure and honest.

One day Lars and Borje gave me a Bible. It was in Persian, my own language. I had never read the Bible in my entire life. I read it with curiosity. I was fascinated by Jesus, by His works and by His words. The stories of Him were very different from the stories of the other prophets. Jesus seemed to be more than what I understood a prophet to be. I could not find any place in the Bible where Jesus killed or fought against anyone. There was no story of any wife and He made no earthly kingdom for Himself. I was fascinated by His love and His many miracles. He raised the dead, healed the deaf and dumb and could give sight back to the blind. There was an authority in His words that no ordinary prophet had. People followed Him not because He had a sword but because of His words. He never sinned. Reading the Bible changed my attitude towards Jesus.

There was a force, an energy in these Christians

which was real. There was a light and purity that I had not seen even in the most fanatic Muslims.

I was very proud of being a Muslim. I did not want to be naive and weak. Islam was a religion of fighting against evil and unrighteousness. I had always hated unrighteousness and loved what was right. I had always considered myself a good man. I never wanted to hurt anyone. I thought that I was living according to the laws of God. I loved God and did what was right, to the best of my knowledge. Yet something strange was happening to me, something I did not understand. The more I got to know these Christians and the more I read the Bible, the less I liked myself. My high thinking about myself was changing. It was as though a veil was being lifted off my eyes and I could see myself more clearly. I saw the real me, and it was not at all attractive. It seemed as though the more I got to know Jesus through the Bible and His followers, the clearer the picture I received of God and of myself. It was like coming into the light from a dark room. The eyes of my understanding were beginning to open.

At the same time an awful fear began to grow within me. A doubt, a voice of warning. What if I were wrong? What if Mohammed was not sent of God? Even the thought of it sent a shiver through my bones. I was afraid of God, afraid of resisting His holy prophet. I would be an infidel who would fall victim of the mighty wrath of God. God would destroy me in the pits of hell.

Who could stand against the God of Islam? Think of what had happened to those who rejected the prophet Mohammed. They were killed and a subject of the curse of God. These were just some of the thoughts which arose to challenge my doubting of my religion.

The more I searched to find the truth, the more the fear increased. I could not sleep at night in a dark room. I had to have a light on. I had nightmares often, and woke up in the middle of the night full of fear. I had always been a very heavy sleeper. Now I would wake up at the slightest sound or movement.

The more I saw of the life of these Christians, their love and purity, the more I was convinced that I was not pure. I had always thought of them as impure people. I would wash my hands after shaking hands with them. I would wash my mouth if I ate their food. But here I was cheating and lying to them and in return they forgave and loved me. I began to see that I was a sinner. I had always believed that sin was only a horrible act like murdering or robbing a bank. I had been able to justify my wrongdoings. If I lied, I called it a "white lie". If I fornicated I counted it as a natural need. Cursing was a normal part of everyone's conversation. The list went on.

My life came into light in contact with these Christians and the Bible. How could the life of these Christians, whose Bible had been changed and whose prophet was before Mohammed, be a better example than mine? How could something false make so many good people? How could they have so much love and forgiveness? How could their eyes shine so brightly? These were the thoughts with which I constantly fought.

But the worst of all was that I no longer liked myself. I was no longer proud of who I was. I felt like an unclean person. How could I be a better person? What could wash me pure? I was envying these Christians' lifestyle. I who had done so many things. I who had kept all the religious laws, the prayers, the fasting and the mourning. I who kept the regulations of eating and drinking. Did anything have the power to change me? I was so confused.

Everything was out of order in my life - my family, my finances, my plans, and now even myself. Would it help to change my religion? What would happen if I were to become a Christian? The idea started to ring its bell in my heart and it scared me to death. "Think of the consequences," I told myself. I would lose my family and friends. My own people would laugh at me. I would be counted as an infidel or a traitor whose just punishment is death. How could I deny and leave Mohammed, the prophet of God? How could Islam be wrong with so many people following it? How could one deny the revelation of Islam? What fear and confusion I had!

Oh, God, what is the truth? Was it possible for a Muslim to become a Christian? Apparently it was! One day I was introduced to a Pakistani who had been converted to Christianity from Islam in Pakistan. As a result he had been committed to a mental hospital by his own father. He escaped and came to Sweden as a refugee. He was the first Muslim convert I had ever heard of. But he had been a Sunni Muslim. I had never heard of any Muslim from Iran being converted! We were Shi'ite, the fanatical ones. If they had done that with a Sunni, what would they do with me?

These thoughts continued for months and my doubts about Islam increased more and more until finally, with total honesty, I made a simple request to God: "Show me the truth."

"God," I said, "I did not choose to be a Muslim. I was taught and told from my earliest childhood that Islam is the way, just like Chinese children learn Buddha is the way. How can I know what the truth is unless You show it to me?" I tried to reason with God peacefully so that He would not get angry with my thinking. "God, I am confused. Everyone claims to be right: the Hindus, Buddhists, Muslims. Which way is the true way to You? They all say that any religion is a way to God, all except Jesus. He said, 'No man can come to the Father except through me'. What if He is right and I am wrong?" I just had to find out the truth. "God," I continued, "I want to try Jesus and if He is not the truth, then I will repent and return to Islam. God, please understand my confusion and not be angry with me if I am acting foolishly."

I knelt by my bedside and prayed in Persian. I said to Jesus, "Jesus, if You are the only way and the Son of God, prove Yourself to me and if I know You are the truth I will follow You even if it costs me my life. Change me, Jesus, forgive me for all my sins."

Not long afterwards I came across these Bible verses: Jesus said, *"Beware of false prophets, who come to you in sheep's clothing, but inwardly they are ravenous wolves. You will know them by their fruits. Do men gather grapes from thorn bushes or figs from thistles? Even so, every good tree bears good fruit; but a bad tree bears bad fruit. A good tree cannot bear bad fruit, nor can a bad tree bear good fruit."*[1] These words of Jesus spoke to me very powerfully. My eyes opened and I could see the fruits. I saw my father, my religious friends, my own life. I saw our fruit. I observed the fruits of my religion throughout history. I had seen it with my own eyes in Iran. I saw the SWORD and I saw BLOOD! Jesus showed it to me. I had been unable to see it with my own eyes. I had tried to figure it out but the result was only confusion. But now I could see! Something happened that day when I knelt and called on the name of Jesus. I was given the ability to see the truth. It was so very simple and easy yet so few could see it. It was as though scales had fallen off my eyes.

One of the hardest things for me had been to accept Jesus as the Son of God. I just could not understand it with my mind. How could God have a son and even if He did, how could people kill His

1. Matthew 7:15-19

Son. The Bible says: *"No one can say, 'Jesus is Lord' except by the Holy Spirit."*[2] Something had happened to me which I could not explain. Suddenly, it was not hard to believe that God sent Jesus to take flesh upon Himself and become a perfect lamb without blemish, a perfect sacrifice, for the sins of the world.

I was now able to understand the Bible, the words of Jesus. I had no doubt in my heart that the Bible was the infallible Word of God, from the beginning to the end. It was like I saw everything in a different light. Somehow I felt that I had been blind and now I had received my sight. The burden I had had was lifted and the confusion was gone.

I'll never forget that day when I woke up and I realized that I no longer needed to do my early morning prayer in Arabic towards Mecca. What a relief it was. I could pray in my own language, at any time, and in any direction I wanted. How happy I was to be free from fasting during the month of Ramadan, especially in Sweden where the sun is up for 22-23 hours a day in summertime. Oh, how wonderfully free I was. Above all, the confusion was gone. Oh, it felt so good!

Have you ever been lost in an unknown place and then after searching and searching you finally found the right way? How did you feel? Relieved? That is what I felt. I could somehow breathe better. I could smell the air. It was like having been in a closed and

2. 1 Corinthians 12:3

dark prison and then being released. The smell was the aroma of freedom. I received new strength. I had a lust for life again. Oh, how wonderful I felt. It felt as though I had been lost in a desert searching for water and now I had found the river of the fresh and living water. It was so refreshing. I could hear the sound of the wind and feel the breeze like never before. It was as though I was born anew, in my soul, in my body and in my heart. My attitude toward people was changed. The hate and bitterness was gone. Before, I had hated some people without any reason. That was all gone. There was a peace and rest in me which was new. I had received joy. It was more than having fun. It was a real joy which I didn't need to express. It was just there. More than anything else I felt completely in love with Jesus. He became so near and so important to me. I could hear Him talk to me through the Bible. When He did, I felt that I was an important person. I did not need to suffer and do good in order to be loved by Him and be close to Him. He was there to lift me up from the pit.

One night as I was reading and meditating on the words of Jesus in the Bible, I read the part when Jesus was with His disciples having the last supper on the night when He was arrested by the hypocrites. *"And He took bread, gave thanks and broke it and gave it to His disciples, saying, 'This is my body given for you; do this in remembrance of me'."*[3] I was meditating

3. Luke 22:19

on this passage of the Bible when I heard Him talking to me. It was not an audible voice, but a gentle voice inside of me that said, "Reza, this was my body broken on the Cross because of you." It was not a condemning voice, it did not make me feel guilty. No, it was a cry of love as I had never heard before. Jesus was so personal to me that it was almost as though I was the only one for whom He had died. I broke into tears and cried like a baby. Full of the joy of God, I felt accepted just as I was, for the first time in my life.

I was so happy about my conversion that I wanted to tell the whole world about it. Sometimes I wanted to stand in public places and cry out to people, "Don't look so miserable! Jesus can change your life!"

I often wondered why I had not known anything about Jesus earlier in my life. Why had I argued so much with the Christians and denied what they said? Where were the Lars' and the Borje's when I used to walk away from home crying to God and wondering if He ever heard me? Why hadn't anyone told me about Jesus during all of those years that I was searching? I had been searching for God. Why weren't there enough Christians in my home country to tell me about Jesus?

I soon started telling people about my faith. I witnessed wherever I could. The Christians would give me 10 to 15 minutes in their meetings to testify, but I often went over time. I enjoyed witnessing to Muslims more than in churches because there was no time limit. And they reacted, they either did not want to listen or they would argue with me for hours.

Many of my old friends laughed and made fun of me. That did not bother me much. I did not care what people thought of me any more, as long as I was accepted by God. I just wanted to give the people of my country, especially Muslims, a chance to hear of the work of my Saviour. I couldn't keep quiet about my faith and my love for Jesus. I guess I told everyone about my conversion, everyone except my family. I was afraid of their reaction.

There was still some fear left in my life even though I had accepted the Lord Jesus and was set free from Islam. One night I had a nightmare. I was half awakened in the middle of the night. The lamp over my bed looked like a weird creature. Something landed on my chest. It felt as if an aeroplane had landed on me. I was very afraid and was shaking and sweating in my bed. I felt the presence of an evil thing. I didn't know what it was but I knew the name of Jesus could set me free. I wanted to cry out Jesus' name but my mouth was frozen. I kept whispering Jesus' name in my mind. Finally, my mouth was loosened and I cried out and rebuked Satan in Jesus' name. The thing left me and I've never had any problem with fear since then.

About a year after my conversion, as I was on my way home, I heard the Lord talking to me. He told me to write to my parents and tell them about my conversion. When I got home I had a letter from my mother in the mail box. I obeyed the Lord and answered my Mother's letter. I wrote a six-page letter to my family telling them of my new faith in Christ. I specifically pleaded with them not to think I was insane. The idea of my becoming a Christian would be completely incomprehensible to them. They would naturally think I had lost my mind. I sent the letter to Iran, and trusted the Lord.

A couple of weeks later I received a phone call from Iran. My elder sister was on the phone. She was very upset and wanted to know if I was okay. She asked me if I had lost my mind. "Are you mad? What do you mean you have become a Christian? A Muslim cannot turn to another religion," she said. "Since Mother received your letter she has been crying and talking to your picture," she continued. "Mum is going crazy because of you, Reza. Wasn't it enough that you left us and broke her heart? Look what you are doing to her now. She could have a heart attack worrying about you, and if Dad finds out about this we will not have peace at home. Repent and turn back. Who are these people who have pressured you to change your religion?" And she went on talking like that for quite a while.

The news of Mother's condition upset me. I did not want to hurt her especially after all she had been through in her life with my father. I prayed to Jesus. It was a difficult time for me.

Not long after my sister's call I received another phone call, this time from the Iranian Consulate in

Stockholm. The consul was on the line and asked me if I was okay physically and mentally. "Yes," I replied, wondering why they were bothering with me. They explained that they had received a telegram from my family which said I was mentally sick and needed to be put under hospital care. Fortunately they took my word for it that I could not have felt better!

Finally, I received a letter from my father. He had found out what had happened. He had disinherited me as his son. I was forbidden to have any contact with my family as long as I confessed to be a Christian. He counted me a traitor. Not only did my family cut me off, but my friends also despised me and accused me of getting paid by the CIA to spread Christianity. Sometimes, jokingly, they would ask me how much they would be paid to become a Christian.

Realizing the risk of ever returning to Iran, I applied for religious assylum in Sweden. I received it. My permanent residency to stay and work was granted in Sweden. I started life anew.

The early years of my faith were difficult. It was a time of training for me. I was being changed and had to learn obedience and tolerance. I had been raised in a religion totally different than the teaching of Christ. God was scraping all the dirt off me. The first two years were like going through a hot furnace to be refined and reshaped. I had to give up that old Reza – the proud, stubborn, self-sufficient, independent, selfish Reza. The list could go on and on. Being changed hurts. It's like taking away all the different pieces which make you who you are. That old me, however, was not really worth holding on to. I was being changed into the likeness of Jesus, the Son of the living God.

One of the areas of my life which God dealt with was my belief about the role of women. I was a very macho type. The Lord dealt with that, however, in His own way. One day when I was attending a short term Bible school in Sweden we had a visiting preacher from America. I enjoyed the teaching of the preacher very much but I did not like to sit under the teaching of his wife and took it upon myself to discuss the matter with the dean of the school. I told him I did not believe God had given women the right to teach me! Needless to say, that discussion ended up with me learning my lesson.

Whenever I was in financial need I prayed to God and told Him of my need. The funny thing was that 90 percent of the time God would speak to a woman to give me the money I needed. He used different people each time. Sometimes they did not know much about me. They would come up to me and say the Lord had told them to give me some money. In the beginning I would not accept it and told them that I would have to pray about it. It was humiliating to get help from a female. I had no choice though, since it was the way God provided for me. God broke my pride and I learned that even women can hear from God. I learned that there isn't any macho male dominance in the kingdom of God. In Christ we are all one.

Time went by and I grew in my faith in Jesus. I learned many lessons about how the kingdom of God works. I learned that I could stand firm on God's Word through any problem in life until I received victory. Instead of running from problems, I could fight and win. And even though it was a rough time of training in many areas of my life, it was also a time of healing. The Lord healed my heart. That is where the major conflicts come from. The Lord took away the rejection, the lack and the emptiness, and filled my heart with joy and peace.

Chapter 5

The Change and the Call

From the very beginning of my faith I was actively sharing with people about Jesus and my faith in Him. Together with the Swedish brothers and some of the Iranian brothers who had also been converted in Sweden, we held weekly Bible study groups. We also visited Muslims and shared the gospel with them.

I loved to study the Bible on my own on different subjects. I would sit up late at night and read and meditate on the Word of God. I do not remember ever reading the Qur'an through to the end. But the Bible was different. It was not dry teaching. It was stories of how Jesus healed and delivered people. I loved to read of how He healed the sick. When I realized Jesus had promised to His followers that they would perform the works that He did I got very excited. I often looked for the sick among those with whom we shared the gospel in order to pray for them.

I took every opportunity I could find to practice my faith, no matter how absurd it seemed. For about six months I worked in a printing office owned by a member of our church. Often, when I was alone in the room printing, I would preach the words of Jesus, which I often meditated on, to that huge printing machine. I would practice sermons on it. One day my boss caught me and, smiling, asked me if the machine was saved yet. Once when he was away for a week visiting his mother in another city the machine broke down. I was alone there to print a monthly magazine for one of the local churches. The machine had broken down previously and my boss had fixed the problem. He told me before he left this time that if it should break down again, I could go home and take the week off until he came back. "But," I thought, "it can't hurt to pray for a machine. If Jesus raised dead people, He can surely raise a dead machine." I laid my hands on the printing machine. Nothing happened, so I gave up the idea and was on my way to the washroom to clean the ink off my hands and go home. I heard the voice of the Lord saying, "Do you really believe I can fix the machine?" I turned around and prayed for it again, this time with faith and expectation. My eyes popped open when I pushed the button and the machine started to run anew. My faith grew stronger in the power of God.

In addition to work I was studying, taking some prerequisite courses in order to enter the Swedish university system. But after studying for three semesters I realised that my heart was no longer in books and school. I decided to take a year off from school and study to serve the Lord on the mission field outside of Sweden.

Lars, the Swedish brother who had led me to the Lord, told me that he and his family had decided to go to Spain to work among the Iranians there. At that time there were one hundred thousand Iranians who had fled from the war between Iran and Iraq and sought refuge in Spain. Lars wanted to spread the gospel of Jesus among them. He asked me if I was interested in joining them and helping out. I told him I would pray about it. I asked the Lord to show me if this was His will.

About a week later I received a letter from an English woman living in Spain who was working with the Christian organization Youth With A Mission. I did not know who she was. I had never even heard her name. She did not know anything about Lars and their plans for going to Spain nor of their asking me to go along. Later I found out that she had heard about me through some believers in England. In her letter she asked me if I would be interested in moving to Spain to help them start a work among Iranian refugees. I was thrilled to receive her letter. I had asked God His will concerning Spain and He had answered very clearly.

I decided to go to Spain during one week of the summer and check out the situation. There I met a group of Iranian believers and some ex-missionaries to Iran. They were there during the summer evangelizing among the Iranians.

That summer many Iranians had an opportunity to hear the healing and forgiving message of Jesus. Since the revolution and the war, many of them had been persecuted and were disillusioned with Islam. Many Persians were denying their faith in Islam which they had always respected so highly. Since the revolution over three million Iranians had fled the country to all parts of the world. It was a very good time to share the hope and love of Jesus with these people from a country closed to missionary work and who were disappointed in religion. I spent one week there and helped the team.

I do not know what it was but my first impression of Spain wasn't good. I didn't like it and on returning to Sweden I decided to forget the idea of moving to Spain and continue my studies at the university instead. I was accepted at the University of Gothenburg on the west coast of Sweden, a city about 350 miles from Stockholm. I moved to Gothenburg and started university. I rented an apartment, bought furniture and the things I needed for my new home.

It was exciting to enrol at one of the most famous universities of Sweden. However, I knew that there was something wrong. My peace was not complete. Sitting in class on the first day was not fun at all. It was a mathematics class. I could not understand what the professor was talking about. My concentration was totally gone. At home in the afternoon in my isolated room I tried to review the lesson but my mind had become blocked, I could not understand the book. It was very strange. The second day at school was the same. I felt so out of place there. That afternoon I tried again to study but it was hopeless. I prayed to the Lord and then I saw what was wrong. I realized that I had disobeyed God. The Lord had called me to Spain, not to Gothenburg. I had missed God by thousands of miles.

I closed the study books that night and asked the Lord for forgiveness. My heart was in Spain even though I did not like it there. The following day I went to school and told the Dean that I was quitting. Was she ever surprised! I sold the books and gave away my furniture to friends. All I kept for myself was a backpack and a suitcase. I bought a train ticket and left for Spain.

Chapter 6

Spain, the Land of the Sun

It was a long three-day trip by train to Spain. When I arrived in Madrid I contacted the English woman and temporarily rented a room at the YWAM base in Madrid. Soon after my arrival an ex-missionary to Iran, who had been part of the summer team, joined me with his family from England. They had also decided to dedicate a couple of years of work among the Iranians in Spain.

We soon started our evangelistic work. The first step was to find the Iranians. We looked around to find the different places where they would gather: the streets, in market places, at cafeterias, in billiard halls and so on. At times we would go to the centre of Madrid with my Persian Bible searching for those who looked like Iranians. We would lay friendly wagers on whether someone was Spanish or Iranian since they can look very much alike. Sometimes I could tell the difference by their way of walking.

My missionary friend and I made a very interesting pair that attracted many people. He was a very English man and I was very Persian. He was tall and skinny. I always had problems keeping up with him when we walked together. He was always ten yards ahead of me. People were attracted by his Persian accent and to the fact that he could speak Persian fluently – a bonus in making contacts with them.

I started to enjoy the Spanish way of life. It was similar in some ways to our eastern culture. I enjoyed the climate and the food. My missionary friend and I were out in the streets until late at night looking for Iranians to witness to. We often discussed religion with them for many hours. If they were interested, we would then arrange for another visit and follow them up.

People had become afraid of any religion because of the consequences they had experienced in Iran. Therefore we tried our best not to look like religious people.

As we were able to locate the places where they gathered, we made many contacts. Some of them invited us to their homes, and made us delicious Persian food. We ate their food and would talk for many hours about Jesus and our faith in Him. If they were interested we would invite them back to our home and cultivate friendships. We sometimes arranged picnics and played many different games. We would pray together with them.

We loved them. That was what they needed. I often sat at a game of chess or backgammon, which is very popular among them. Sometimes I played billiards in order to make contact and show love and friendship. If I could win the game they would want to play again and I could talk more about Jesus. I wanted to do everything in my power and the power of God to win them for Christ. We did not want to act as religious and dry people whose love would be offered only in exchange for their salvation.

Being together with the English brother who had lived in Iran for nine years and could speak fluent Persian was a bonus of course. People wanted to know why he was interested in them. Often we were invited to different homes and were offered several foods of Persian hospitality. To be invited to a Persian home is a sign of trust and that was a good start for us to share the gospel of Jesus Christ. They enjoyed our friendship and we enjoyed their cooking!

We met people from all classes of society: rich and poor, fanatical Muslims and secular Muslims, Armenians and Bahai's, Communists and atheists. Some of them had been in prison, others in the war. Some of them had lost their families and others, everything they owned. They were people marked with the scars of the fanaticism of a religion. We listened to them and told them that there was one who cared and who had the power to heal and set them free.

These Iranian refugees were in need of love and acceptance. They had lost their pride and self-assurance. It is easier for an Iranian to lose his life than his pride. Many of them had fled for their lives with their families and left behind all they had. They did not want to be called refugees. They did not want to feel left out or to be the object of racism and spite. Yet they did want to tell the story of the hardships they had been through. Some of them had no contact with the Spaniards because they could not speak the language. Many of them were isolated. They did not even have contact with their own countrymen because of the lack of trust. They had been burned by the revolution, and their stories, though in some cases almost unbelievable, were very real. They often talked about what they had been through with a voice of sorrow and despair.

As a messenger of Christ I made no discrimination of race, religion or background. I became friends with Jews, Bahai's, Muslims, Communists and Armenians. As a Muslim I had hated and despised the majority of these people. I would not, as a Muslim, touch a Christian or a Jew or a Bahai. I had hated the Communists and the atheists with a passion. As a teenager in Iran I would wash my hands each time I played with our Christian neighbour. When our downstairs Jewish neighbour sent us different cakes and cookies we would never eat them. We counted it as unclean. But now here I was loving them from the bottom of my heart and crying to God for their salvation and peace. I visited with them, went to their homes, ate their food. I often stayed overnight at their homes and listened to their stories until the small hours of the morning. They made me food and I would find a place to sleep on their couch.

I knew that only the love of Jesus could bind their sores and heal their broken hearts. I knew that once they received Jesus into their lives they would be refreshed and find new strength. As the Bible says, *"Repent, therefore and be converted, that your sins may be blotted out, so that times of refreshing may come from the presence of the Lord."*[1] They needed a time of refreshing, a new desire for life, a new start. I knew Jesus would save them once they gave their hearts to Him. I wanted to reach as many of them as possible. I wanted to tell them about the Saviour. Just as He had saved me from despair, He could do the same for them. I had a hope and I wanted them to know that they could have it too if they believed.

The conditions under which refugees lived in Spain were some of the worst in all Europe. The government was not able to take care of them. Very few ever received their residency status as far as we knew. The government did not provide any social help except through the Red Cross, from which they received a small amount each month. Because of the high rate of unemployment already existing in Spain they were not able to find work. This is one of the reasons why some of them became involved in prostitution and drugs. Almost every one of them was trying to find refuge in North America or other European countries.

An organization was established by the name IRC[2] which helped the refugees to seek assylum in the United States. I was able to get a job as an

1. Acts 3:19
2. International Rescue Committee.

interpreter with the IRC. Through this work I came into contact with many more Iranians with whom I could share the good news of the gospel of Jesus. This was the reason I applied for the job. It was also a financial help for me for a while.

Living in Spain was a step of faith for me. I had to trust God for my needs every month. Lars sent me some money from Sweden but that only covered half of my expenses. Every month I cried out to God for help. I learned that the only way was to believe God. I was not sent by any missionary organization, so the only way to live was to believe God. That was what God wanted too. I could not teach people to trust God if I myself failed to do so. It was not easy but it worked every time. I learned not to worry but only believe. Of course there were times when I only ate bread and tea. That was all I could afford. However, I did not give up trusting God.

I remember one day I was very badly in need of money. All I had was 35 pesetas and that was not enough to get me to work by the subway. That day I had to believe God. I prayed and asked Him to send me 5,000pts. (US$40) so I could eat and get by before receiving my paycheck from IRC. I walked around the city park and thanked God for that 5,000pts. which I did not yet have. The Bible says, *"Faith is being sure of what we hope for and certain of what we do not see."*[3] Of course, I could have borrowed from friends but I refused to put my trust

3. Hebrews 11:1

in man. I would rather die of hunger with faith in Jesus than live in riches without having faith in Him. As I was walking I found one peseta on the ground. Then, in my simple faith I said to the Lord, "Thank you, Lord, for the 4,999 pesetas which are left." That day I was invited to food and transport by a friend without her knowing anything of my need. The following day I received a notice from the bank which said I had received 22,000 pesetas from Sweden. Hallelujah! That day I was the happiest man in the whole of Spain. My faith worked and each month I learned more and more about the principles of faith.

I practised my faith not only in finance but also in other areas of my life. An apartment was lent to us by a charismatic church in Madrid so that we could hold our weekly Bible studies for the Iranians. It was located in a very old neighbourhood in the centre of Madrid. The building was very old and rusty. The apartment was located on the second floor of the building. The walls were broken, the floor was tilted and the kitchen looked like a half sunken ship with its floor leaning downwards. It was very cold in the winter because there was no way to keep the heat inside. Looking down on the back patio one could see the fallen pieces of concrete from the walls. The only advantage with this house was that it was very central for our outreach. I lived there by myself to host our Iranian friends and of course, it was a cheap place to live.

One day, as I was sitting in the bathroom, I was

looking at the ceiling and was lost in my thoughts. I was staring at the chipped and splintered parts and was wondering what I would do if the house collapsed. All of a sudden the ceiling of the bathroom came crashing down, all except for the part directly above where I was sitting. I thought the house was falling down. I ran out of the bathroom naked calling on the name of Jesus. The hand of the Lord protected me and I was not hurt. We were, however, required by the authorities to evacuate the place. We were able to rent a church and continue our meetings and I rented a room in another place, not much warmer, but a lot safer.

As time went by we got to know many Iranians and many visited our meetings. Some wanted to get to know us, others just wanted help with papers. Many of these visitors were searching for the truth and were honest, even though we did have people come to see us in order to argue, make fun or to spy on us. As we continued, the Lord blessed our work and many received Jesus into their hearts.

Working with these people was not an easy task. One needed all the fruits of the Spirit that there are, especially patience, gentleness and longsuffering, to establish a group of believers among them. It was unlike any other group I've ever seen. We needed the grace of God and He gave it to us. The majority of them were anything but religious.

In our group we had people like Babak and Wzat. She was Bahai and he was a secular Muslim bound by gambling. Then there was Sima, who was stubborn and constantly arguing that Islam was better. Jalil had spent two years in the war between Iran and Iraq and often caused quarrels in the group. Mohammed was a backslidden Christian who had Mob connections and Mojdeh was suspicious of everyone in the group. Shamaz argued and often talked behind our backs. Valin was Armenian and hungry for the Lord but his wife Shiba was half Muslim and half Christian. Masoud did not like me and Ziba was a sad woman whose brother had been executed in prison in Iran and whose wife was still in prison. Jala was very quiet and no one ever knew where he stood. Mahin lied often and Golam lost his money on jackpot machines. Akbar said he had been with Mojahedin and had assassinated over twenty people. He also caused a lot of quarrels. Fereshteh and Sharareh were good people but did not want to give up their old life. Mansur was indifferent but Mina was humble. Mehdi was a genius in discussions. He was very intellectual and the son of a fanatic writer in Iran. Silvia was very helpful but confused. Afsaneh was very serious. Joan was known as a crying woman because she lost everything. Dariush was half mad; one never knew if he spoke truth or lies. Nadom was a foreigner with a broken Persian accent and hard to trust. Berit and her family made good food but were not very interested in spiritual things. Hassan was more interested in karate. There were others, each with a peculiar lifestyle.

These were some of the people who accepted Jesus during the two years of my work in Madrid. Putting them together and making a church out of them was a miracle of God. Sometimes I wondered if God wanted to give up on them. With one exception, they all came from a non-Christian background. They had no knowledge of a Christian life-style whatsoever. To walk in the darkness was the only 'light' they knew. Even the hardest atheists in the West have had some knowledge of Christ in their lives. The only truth these people knew about Jesus was that He was born of the Virgin Mary. But to God be all the glory for the things He did with them. Once they got to know Jesus and dwelt in His Word, they became new creations. Their lives and lifestyles were changed. God was working in them. They grew more and more to maturity in faith in Christ. Each of them can testify to the power of God in their lives.

Working with these people for two years was a school of learning for me. I learned more about love, patience, grace and the power of God. It was good to see the fruit of our labour, to witness first-hand that for Jesus there was no impossible case. It made me strong and bold about the saving power of the Lord. I was proud of these little ones. They were like my children. I felt like a father responsible for their souls even though I was younger than most of them in age. It was like shepherding the flock of God. I did not want any of them to miss the grace of God. I prayed for them and thought of them constantly. They had become my daily life. It was not an occupation but a way of life. I learned more from those two years about the service of the Lord and the ministry than from any books I've read or teaching I've ever received. During that time the Lord destroyed most of the selfishness, pride, self-consciousness and arrogance in my life. I learned in practice the teaching of Jesus. I was not living for myself any more but for Him who gave His life for me. Jesus had crucified that old Reza on His Cross. A new person had risen who loved God not only in words but in the reality of His Word. A person who was not bloodthirsty and full of hate, but one who was constantly cleansed in the blood of Jesus, the perfect Lamb of God. As the Bible says, *"Therefore, if anyone is in Christ, he is a new creation, old things have passed away: behold all things have become new."*[4] Oh, how my heart rejoices for Jesus. He has become everything to me.

4. 2 Corinthians 5:17

Chapter 7

My Other Half!

The Lord had assured me that He would meet all of my needs as long as I was in His plan. One of these needs, of which I often reminded the Lord, was to establish my own family. I had seen the life of my family in Iran and I wanted to have a blessed family, where the peace and joy of God would rest. I asked God for the right girl. Before going to Spain I had met some good Christian girls but I could not get God to agree with my choices. Before my faith in Jesus, God had not been involved in my choice of a wife, but now I was dependent on Him to pick the right girl. The problem was that whenever I fell in love with a girl, I had no peace about marrying her. Therefore I knew God had the right person for me and I just needed to wait for her.

My English co-worker and I had found out about a Lutheran church in Madrid which was helping the Iranian refugees. The church was giving out food and clothing to the refugees one day a week. They needed our help with interpretation. It was a good opportunity for us to come into contact with new people. One day we went there to help them and meet new

Iranians. There were also other people there from other countries to help with the work.

As we were preparing sandwiches a beautiful girl walked in. She was an American missionary working among the illiterate Spaniards. As she walked across the room and we were introduced, the Spirit of the Lord whispered in my heart, "This is your wife." At first I did not like her. I thought she was an arrogant American. But since I knew no Spanish I had to work with her. She would interpret from Spanish to English and then I would interpret from English to Persian and then back again. We helped this church every Thursday.

After a couple of weeks I realized that I was becoming more willing to go to that church and help the refugees. I also realized that it was not only the Iranians who drew me there but also this American girl named Marilyn.

One Thursday after working in the church, I invited Marilyn to have a cup of coffee with me. I wanted to know more about her work. She was hesitant at first but then she accepted my invitation and we walked to a coffee shop in the centre of Madrid called "Lucky".

Thursdays became a very exciting day for me. After working we would go to Lucky's and have coffee with *churros*.[1] I started to like Marilyn very much. One day she asked me to join a Thanksgiving party at her place together with her American friends. I bought a

1. A deep-fat fried donut type pastry.

74

plant and went to her apartment. Her friends could not help noticing my "love-sick" puppy eyes. From that day we met each other more often. According to her it did not take long before I proposed to her. However, it took much longer before she said "yes".

Marilyn wanted to be sure that it was the will of God. I asked the Lord for all kinds of signs to prove to her that God did want us to get married. I knew the Lord had heard my prayer. And then one day we had lunch with a young missionary couple from America. They told us the story of how they met. It was as though we were a carbon copy of them. That was my "Lucky Day". Marilyn accepted my proposal and called home to America to tell them the good news.

We knew that the work among the Iranians in Spain would be for a limited time since the majority of them were moving on to other countries and the time had come for me to leave the work in Madrid and move on too. The brother with whom I worked continued on after I left.

My fiancé and I moved to America to get married in her home town. I was happy to avoid the customs and traditions of getting married in Iran. It was much easier in America, not to mention that in America the bride's family is responsible for the wedding. That was all right with me. I was a broke missionary.

My wife comes from a simple farm family from the suburbs of Philadelphia. They all love the Lord and want to serve Him. I was so grateful to the Lord for giving me such a new family who love Jesus. He had heard my prayer.

Chapter 8

The World, Our Mission Field

Those five hours were one of the coldest bus rides I've ever taken in my entire life. The bus was driving through the mountains of western Romania, stopping in different villages. The seat next to me became free and I called Evert to come and sit there. It was warmer there than in the front of the bus. Evert is the leader of a music group called Zoe who often accompany me on evangelistic campaigns in different countries. The Lord first spoke to my heart concerning Romania when Evert and I were in Poland during the summer of 1988.

I first met Evert in the Fall of 1986 in the city of Gothenburg. After spending the year following our marriage in Bible School in America, I'd returned now with Marilyn to Sweden. I just knew the Lord wanted us there. We moved to Stockholm, and together again with Lars, we started travelling to different cities, preaching in refugee camps and also in local churches.

We had a series of meetings together with Lars in the city of Gothenburg. Evert and his group were leading the worship. The Spirit of the Lord came over me and I started prophesying over him. I had no idea that the Lord would bring our paths together in His service one day.

The following summer I held my first tent campaign in the capital city of Stockholm. As we were planning, the Lord reminded me of the music group Zoe. I invited them to lead the worship for the two week campaign. Since then we have been travelling around the world and holding evangelistic campaigns in different countries.

Here we were now in the December of 1988 travelling again to another Eastern European country to preach the Word of God. We visited various cities and churches during the nine days we were there. We travelled by plane, train and were now travelling 170km by bus, a journey that took five long hours.

We finally arrived at the entrance to the city of Oradea in western Romania. The streets were dark. We had hoped someone from the church would meet us at the bus station but no one was there. We were terribly tired, hungry and cold.

We decided to go on ahead to the assistant pastor's house by taxi. The pastor and his wife welcomed us very warmly and she generously prepared a meal of schnitzel for us. Though I'm not used to eating pork, I just swallowed it down, telling myself with each mouthful "This is beef!" When we arrived in Romania, we hadn't been able to find any food except pork, so for two days I'd eaten only bread. But now I didn't care what food it was. I was hungry! I often tell Evert that he is a better missionary than I am because he eats everything!

After dinner and fellowship with the pastor, he took us to a hotel because they were not allowed to keep foreign guests after 10pm.

This hotel was better than others in which we had stayed in Romania. It was heated and had hot water. That night we did not need to sleep with our sweaters and long-johns on. We slept well and were picked up the next morning for church, well rested, ready for what God had in store for Oradea.

This particular church in Oradea has one of the largest memberships in the country. The building itself could seat approximately 2,500 persons. We were given one meeting in the morning service and one in the evening. The building was full for the morning service and the presence of God was very tangible. People were broken before the Lord and in tears as they heard the Word of the Lord. I announced that we would pray for the sick in the evening meeting.

That evening we arrived at the church half an hour early in order to pray with the other pastors. Already the church was full beyond capacity and people were standing outside pushing to get in away from the cold. We made our way to the office in the church's backyard. The pastor was a little nervous. There were still crowds of people coming. When it was time for the service to begin we followed the pastor back through the crowd in the yard into the back of the church. Once inside though, we then had to reach the altar in the front of the church. Considering the crowd, it was easier said than done. There wasn't even room to breathe. We sucked in our breath trying to make ourselves as small as possible. The pastor went first, Evert followed him carrying his guitar over his head, and I followed Evert. The pastor lost his jacket button because of the pressure of the crowds.

The meeting started with prayer and Evert took over with his guitar, singing in English. I sat on the platform on a small bench behind the pulpit next to my interpreter and the pastor. From the baptismal pool behind us I could feel a cold draught. Yet the whole atmosphere was filled with Jesus and His Holy Spirit. I knew in my heart that Jesus was going to do mighty miracles among these needy people. People were there with great expectation. There were about 4,000 people that night packed in and jammed together. There were hundreds more waiting outside in the freezing cold. Then Evert sang my favourite song, *The Name of Jesus*.

This song always breaks me before the Lord. How sweet and wonderful was the presence of my Jesus, He who has become everything to me. He was truly the only song that brought me joy. How Jesus changed my life. How grateful I was to Him. I was in tears before the Lord, filled with love for Him. Being in His presence those minutes before beginning to preach was better than life. I thought back on how as a Muslim I had longed for a time like this. How

I had been thirsty and hungry for God. How I had tried to please God. Tears were running down my face. I bowed my head and prayed. I prayed for power and blessings of the Spirit of God over the people.

When the song finished, I stood and preached on Ezekiel 34: 15-30: *"I will seek the lost, bring back the scattered, bind up the broken and strengthen the sick . . ."*

The presence of God was so tangible. Many people were in tears, even my interpreter was crying as he interpreted. Several people accepted Jesus into their hearts and then we prayed for the sick.

Jesus did not just give good teaching to people but He also helped them. He healed the sick, fed the hungry, raised the dead, gave sight to the blind. He opened deaf ears, gave strength to lame legs, set people free from the power of Satan, and He forgave the sinners. When Jesus was criticized by the hypocrites for healing a paralyzed man on the sabbath day, He told them, *"My Father has been working until now, and I have been working."*[1] I knew in my heart as I witnessed hundreds of times in our meetings that the Lord was going to heal many of these hurting Romanians of their infirmities. I knew God was still at work. God is not unemployed!

There were so many needs among these Romanians. They prayed and cried out to God and their cries reached His throne of grace. As we were praying they brought a young girl to me who had been born a

1. John 5:17

deaf-mute. She was very afraid and crying loudly. I commanded the deaf and dumb spirit to come out of that little girl in the name of Jesus. All of a sudden she stopped crying and she could hear the prayers of the people. When she started repeating words after me people started shouting and praising God. Jesus was so wonderful and healed so many people. The joy of God had filled the whole atmosphere. Several people were lame and crippled and Jesus healed them. Among them there was a boy who had been crippled in half his body for ten years. The power of God was there. Even people who were standing outside in the cold were healed. People were trying to push forward through the crowds to receive the laying on of hands and prayer.

The pastor asked us to close the meeting or we would have been there all night. I would not have minded being there all night. Apparently, though, he was fearful of government security. They were persecuted constantly. How these people have been oppressed by the cruel dictatorship. Oh what a compassion Jesus had for these people. What a joy in my heart to see Jesus manifesting His love among them! I obeyed the pastor and asked people to pass their handkerchiefs forward so that we could lay hands on them for the sick. Huge piles of handkerchiefs, hats and scarfs were thrown forward to be prayed over.

Ten months later, on my second visit to that church, the pastor told me, "For three months after your visit people came every Tuesday and testified of healings which took place that night."

The Bible says: *"And there are also many other things Jesus did which, if they were written one by one, I suppose that even the world itself could not contain the books that would be written."*[2]

During that trip we visited different cities in which Jesus did the same work. He healed the sick, saved the sinners, set people free from the captivity of Satan and restored many lives from darkness.

What a privilege it was for me to share Jesus with these thirsty and brokenhearted people. How grateful I was to Him to be His ambassador of good tidings. Oh, Hallelujah!

2. John 21:25

Chapter 9

The Life

It was raining cats and dogs. Dusk was approaching as we were driving back to Madrid from Toledo. I had taken my mother, sister and Marilyn on a day's outing to see some historical places in the areas surrounding Madrid.

The year was 1984 and I had been working a year in Spain. It had been four years since I'd last seen any of my family and now my mother and older sister had come to visit me. It was the first time they had wanted to see me after I had become a Christian. Still believing I'd gone mad, they wanted to see me personally.

My sister cried out, "Please stop the car somewhere! My time for the afternoon Namaz (prayer) is about to end," she added. There were no buildings or shelters in sight but she insisted she could do the prayer out in the rain. It was strange to see Behjad so fanatic. Of all my brothers and sisters she was the least interested in practicing religion when I had lived in Iran. However, the Islamic Revolution had affected everyone in one way or another. I respected her beliefs even though I did not believe that way any more. However, I did tell her of her hypocrisy. "What good does it to you if you show your good deeds in front of people's eyes when you will not show them what's in your heart?" I said to her.

I stopped the car and she climbed out and prayed in the pouring rain. She did not know where Mecca was so she guessed. She was soaking wet from the rain by the time she had finished her hasty half-done prayers. Yet I did admire her commitment. I wished many Christians would have the commitment that Muslims have.

My mother and sister stayed with me for 20 days. They had a close-up view of my new life in Christ. They joined our Bible study group which met in my home. Behjad would often start a discussion at the end of my preaching. Since she was pro-Khomeini she would get into arguments with the Mojahedin[1] people who came to our group. They hated each other deeply. They yelled at each other and would accuse each other of different things. One day one of the young men who was very interested in the message of the Bible told them: "Here you are, two Muslims fighting with one another and thirsty for each other's blood. Look at these Christians," he said, "and learn of their love and forgiveness."

We spent many hours sitting and talking, catching up on the family, but I would not let them talk negatively about anyone. "It is impossible for a well to give both sweet and salt water," I told them. My

1. A leftist Muslim group in violent opposition to the Khomeini regime.

sister told me later that when she went back to her work in Iran, she had put a sign on top of her office desk which said "In this room, backbiting is not permitted!". People were surprised that she had became holier in spite of visiting the West.

Praise the Lord! My new life had had an impact on my family, even though they refused to accept Jesus in their lives. My Mum was especially touched by the new way I was living. She was so happy that all of my confusion and emptiness was gone. One day the Lord healed her hand of rheumatism when I prayed for it in the name of Jesus. Since then, she always asks me to pray if she has important prayer requests. "The Lord hears your prayers," she says.

In 1986, two years after my mother and sister visited me, I met my elder brother in West Germany, and five years after that first visit with Mum, I had a visit with my Dad in Singapore in 1989. Even though I had been rejected by my brother and disinherited by my father, the love of Jesus had always been warm in my heart towards them. My father said to me one day, "You are my luckiest child. Your family is the happiest among us."

Thank God for Jesus. It is all because of Him. The Bible says, *"He who has the Son has life; he who does not have the Son of God does not have life."*[2] A well-known Swedish singer who accepted Jesus said to me one day, "I had existence before I met Jesus, now I have life." The Bible says, *"In Him was life, and that life was the light of men."*[3] As the water comes

2. 1 John 5:12
3. John 1:4

from the well so life comes only through the Son, Jesus the Messiah. "Before I met Jesus I did not know that the birds sing so beautifully," said an Iranian woman who accepted Jesus as her Saviour.

I have seen how people struggle to have peace and joy in life. I saw it in my own life how I searched for a meaningful life. I saw it in my own family. I witnessed it in the lives of my relatives and close friends. Without Jesus there is no life, only existence. David said, in the book of Psalms, *"For with you is the fountain of life."*[4] If you are looking for a meaning in life, if you want to live a life with God you have to go to the fountain. Jesus is the fountain of life. One day Jesus stood and said in a loud voice, *"If anyone is thirsty, let him come to ME and DRINK."*[5] The water that He gives you will refresh your body, soul and your spirit.

You may ask, how can one drink from the fountain of life? Only by faith. Will you drink it NOW?

4. Psalm 36:9
5. John 7:37

Chapter 10

The Name

As soon as we had prayed together and he had received Jesus into his heart he fell face down onto the table and was totally gone. Then the Spirit of the Lord told me to stand up and preach and pray for the sick.

We were in a Christian café on the south coast of Spain. I had taken a group of Bible school students from Uppsala in Sweden for two weeks of evangelism in Spain. In the mornings we would go out and have street meetings and at night we would invite people to the café and talk to them individually.

Tommy, one of the students, would often find Muslims from North Africa and bring them to me. He would tell them that it is possible for a Muslim to be converted to Christ, because he had a friend that was. This time he had brought me a man by the name of Mustafa from Morocco.

We sat around a table in the Christian café and talked for several hours with Mustafa. He was very open to the gospel and after I had explained to him how he could receive the life of Jesus he was willing to accept Him as his Lord and Saviour. So we prayed the prayer of Salvation together. As soon as we were finished he was knocked down onto the table by the Spirit of the Lord. I stood up in the café and started to preach about the power of the name of Jesus as the Lord commanded me. I then prayed for the sick in the name of Jesus and the Lord healed as many as came forward for prayer. There was great joy in that place.

I went back to my table to check on my newly converted friend. He still lay with his face on the table. I lifted his head, "How are you doing, Mustafa?" I asked him.

"There are snakes everywhere," he answered, "They are crawling all over me." I knew there were demons actively trying to scare this man from his faith in Jesus. I turned to him and with a firm voice commanded the unclean spirits to leave him in the name of Jesus. As soon as the name "Jesus" was out of my mouth, Mustafa was thrown to the ground and began crawling around like a snake. He was unconscious of what he was doing. He was pulling his hair and was trying to pull his socks off. As a body-builder he had strong muscles. Mustafa was struggling. He tore his undershirt into pieces as he was crawling on his stomach. We turned him over and I pulled his shirt open so that he would not strangle himself. He was clawing at his body while the demons were torturing the poor man and they would not come out.

I cried out to the Lord, "What shall we do?"

"Let everyone leave the room," the Lord answered.

I asked everyone to leave except my interpreter. People wanted to stay and see what would happen, but I told them they had to leave the room. A miracle cannot happen in an atmosphere of unbelief. When everyone had left I cried out aloud, "In the name of Jesus Christ of Nazareth the Son of the living God, I command you unclean and foul spirits to leave this man!" I then heard Mustafa mumbling something in French. I asked my interpreter what he meant.

"He says, 'stop it'," was the reply.

I cried out again, "I will not stop until you all come out of him and leave him alone." All of a sudden Mustafa started to yawn. He stood up, conscious again, and felt very hot. We took him to the men's room and he threw water all over his body. He said he felt very lightened and relaxed. Since he was still weak we gave him something to eat and drink. We later walked him home. Mustafa was so happy. He said to me that he felt as if he had been washed in perfume. Glory be to God! What a great testimony to the saving power in the name of Jesus.

I have often witnessed how demons bow before the name of Jesus and obey. How wonderfully people can receive freedom and salvation in that Name. The name of "Jesus" means "the one who saves". The Bible says: *"Nor is there salvation in any other, for there is no other name under heaven given to men by which we must be saved."*[1] I do not know of any name that

1. Acts 4:12

can defeat the forces of Satan except the name of Jesus. Under heaven there is only one name by which man can be saved - the holy name of JESUS!

An Iranian Muslim convert once told me of how he had accepted Jesus while in prison in Iraq. He was in the war fighting against Iraq. He was captured, imprisoned and tortured by the Iraqi forces. In prison he was able to get hold of some pills and decided to finish his misery by putting an end to his life. Just before he swallowed the tablets he heard a voice from heaven: "Call on the name of Jesus," it repeated. He obeyed and whispered the name of Jesus.

"As soon as I did, the burden was lifted from my heart and I received the desire to live again," he explained. Soon afterwards he was set free from prison and came to Sweden. There, in the refugee camp he heard the message of the Gospel and gave his life to Jesus.

The Bible says: "*Everyone who calls on the name of the Lord will be saved.*"[2] You can be free and receive the salvation of God if you will only believe and call upon the name of Jesus. Will you call upon Him now?

2. Romans 10:13

Chapter 11

The Blood

It was the second time I'd phoned home. "Are you okay?" I asked my wife.

"Nothing yet," she answered.

It was Friday night and we had a "prayer mountain" in the church. Friday nights are dedicated to prayer in our church. That's why it's called "the prayer mountain." I had gone to the church to pray as I usually do on Fridays when I am at home and not travelling.

My wife and I were expecting our first child. It could come any minute. Earlier in the evening Marilyn had felt some contractions but they were not very regular. I decided to go to the prayer mountain and call home every ten minutes to find out if anything was happening.

It was an exciting time for me. The Lord had blessed me with a good wife. And here I was waiting for our first child. After ten minutes I went out to call again. This time she said something was going on. The contractions were coming at closer intervals. I rushed into the church and told my pastor that I was going to the hospital. I drove home quickly and took my wife to the hospital.

The nurse checked her out and assured us that there would be quite a wait. She gave Marilyn some pills to help her sleep and sent us home. By 1 am contractions were still keeping her awake, so we phoned the hospital and they said to come on in. Again the nurse said there was a long wait ahead but since we had been there earlier they let us stay overnight.

Marilyn was in pain off and on and I was needed there to help her breathe. As is the custom in Sweden, the father is present through the process of childbirth. We had to take special classes together to learn how to relax and how to breathe during the birth process. I was very tired since it was now 4 o'clock in the morning and nothing had yet happened. I lay down on the other bed in the room and was able to get a couple of hours sleep. Marilyn looked exhausted when I awoke. I could not do much except encourage her and pray.

By 1 o'clock in the afternoon we knew the final stage was coming. The contractions were getting more and more intense, and we were fighting together to breathe right. Even though I was not the one going through that awful pain, I could still feel it. We fought for three hours and finally the midwife said it was time.

I felt some kind of "unease" in my spirit. I did not know what it was. I did not know if it was my tiredness or if my spirit was sensitive to something wrong. Honestly, I did not trust the midwife. She looked nervous. Marilyn did not use any painkiller so she was screaming at the top of her voice. I stood beside her and held her hand and tried to labour together with her.

Suddenly, there it was! I saw the head of the baby out! I cried out in joy and praised the Lord. What a love came over me all of a sudden for the baby. I didn't know what to say or do, to shout, scream, laugh or cry. Marilyn screamed one last hard scream and the baby was born.

The midwife was still very nervous. So was I. She hit the head of the baby on the table before I cut the cord. I was glad she did not drop the baby.

It was a girl. She was beautiful and I was so proud. The midwife put her on Marilyn's chest. After a while another lady came to clean her. She took the baby, and I went with them to the other room. She started cleaning the baby and checking her out. She counted her fingers and toes. She checked her mouth and looked at me. Something was wrong. She looked at me half sad and told me that the baby had no upper palate in her mouth and her chin was short. She tried to comfort me with words of human pity. I told her not to worry about it. I did not want to concentrate on her unbelief. The Bible says that a righteous man shall live by faith and not by what he sees or feels. Of course I felt sad but deep inside I believed God and tried to overcome the emotions of self-pity. As far as I am concerned, self-pity is sin because it is unbelief, and I hate unbelief. I told the nurse that everything would be okay. She handed me the baby and I went back to our room, to Marilyn. I laid the baby on her back in a crib at the bottom of the bed and sat next to Marilyn on the bed. I told her what the nurse had told me and tried to comfort her.

The midwives and nurses left us alone to talk and eat a sandwich. Suddenly I felt I had to check on the baby. I looked at her and ran out to the nurse's station. There was something wrong with her. The baby's face had turned blue and there was white foam coming from her nose and mouth. She looked lifeless. The midwife ran back with me to the room and looked at the baby. She grabbed her and shook her with her head down. The midwife looked very worried and ran out to the corridor with the baby and yelled for help. All the nurses ran toward us in the corridor and she told them that the baby was not breathing.

In those few moments I felt as if the whole of hell had come against me. The baby's tongue had fallen back in her throat, gotten caught in the cleft palate, and blocked her breathing. I thought of all those nine months of pregnancy. I thought back to how I laid my hands on Marilyn's stomach and had prayed for the baby every night. I thought of all the discomfort that my wife had gone through for the past nine months. I felt so heavy in my heart.

The midwives were hovering over the baby, trying to bring her tongue forward and give her oxygen.

Meanwhile I stood in the corner of that room and lifted my hands to God and prayed in other tongues. I did not listen to the devil. I turned to God and believed Him for a miracle.

As I was praying in the Spirit, the Spirit of the Lord talked to me about the blood of Jesus. Jesus said that when the Holy Spirit comes He will help and comfort you and tell you the whole truth. That was exactly what He was doing. My eyes were lifted up from that room and became focussed on the Cross of Jesus. He had won victory for me on that Cross. The Holy Spirit reminded me of the blood of the Passover in the Old Testament.

The night before the Israelites were released from the captivity of Pharaoh, the Lord told them to sacrifice a lamb and take its blood and spread it on the sides and tops of the doorframes of their houses. That night every firstborn of that land died except those whose homes had been covered by the blood of the Lamb.[1] The blood kept them safe. Death could not pass through. That Passover lamb was only a type of the perfect sacrifice that was to come, Jesus, the perfect Lamb of God.

I said to the devil: "I do not only have the blood of the Lamb of God on my house, but I have it sprinkled all over me and my family." As I started thanking God for the blood of Jesus, faith arose in me. I rebuked the spirit of death and I gave God the glory. The unease left me and the peace of God

1. Exodus 12

descended on my heart. I saw the midwife coming towards me. She was smiling.

"She'll be okay," she said.

"I know it!" I responded. And I did!

A couple of days later that same midwife came to visit us and brought our baby a doll. She'd been touched by the love of Jesus.

Thank God for the blood of Jesus. His blood does not remind us of revenge or the sweet memory of a martyr. No, it is the life-giving blood. It is the living blood. It started to run out of Jesus' broken body on the Cross two thousand years ago. But it did not stop there; it is still flowing to bring us life. If you believe in that pure and holy blood of Jesus you can also receive life. Jesus said: *"Whoever . . . drinks my blood, has eternal life, and I will raise him up at the last day."*[2]

In medicine they transfuse blood from a healthy person to a dying one. That person can receive new strength and return to life. Jesus was the only man in the whole of history who was without any sin. He was the only healthy man. We humans from the four corners of this Earth are guilty of many sins. We are the sick ones. We all need the blood of Jesus if we want life. As our blood is the life of the flesh, so the blood of Jesus is the life of our souls. If you drink it you will have the eternal life He has promised.

How can one drink of the blood that was shed two thousand years ago? Through faith! To drink of that blood is to believe that it is the only way of

2. John 6:53,54

redemption and forgiveness for your sins. Jesus said: *"He who . . . drinks my blood, abides in me, and I in him."*[3] Will you drink it now?

3. John 6:56

Chapter 12

A Simple Message

Today people all over the world are trying to cover their sins by doing good, by keeping the regulations of their religion. They try to cover their guilt and sinful conscience by doing what they believe to be good works. They pray, they fast, they give to the poor, and so on. Yet deep inside they know they are guilty. Man is born with guilt and sin.[1] There is no man-made cure for the guilty conscience. When Pilate, the Roman governor of Judea, condemned Jesus to be crucified, he asked for water to wash his hands of the sin he was committing.[2] Sin cannot be washed away by water. I myself was trying to wash and cover my sin for many years with the water of religion. There is only one cure and answer for sin. There is only one remedy which can cleanse the sin of man - the blood of Jesus, the Son of the living God.[3]

Jesus did not come to help us cover our sins. He came to wipe them away. ". . . *But now, once in the end of the ages He has appeared to put away sin by the*

---

1. Romans 5:12
2. Matthew 27:24
3. Hebrews 9:22

101

sacrifice of Himself."[4] Jesus offered Himself as a sacrifice for the sin of the world, a perfect lamb, the propitiation for our sins. Religion cannot make that sacrifice. They can be a copy or a type but the real and the true sacrifice was made only by the Lamb of God, Jesus the Christ. To receive Jesus as the one and only sacrifice for our sin is to receive the testimony of God. To reject Jesus is to reject the only way which God has provided for man to be washed and forgiven of his sins.

The reason I have written this book is to testify of this great sacrifice of God. My desire is to convince you of this truth. There is only one God and one truth. Jesus said: *"You will know the truth, and the truth will set you free."*[5]

You may ask, "What is truth?" There is only one answer to that. Truth is Jesus and Jesus is the truth! Everything outside of Jesus is a mirage. Jesus is the only one who has ever proclaimed: *"I am the way and the truth and the life."*[6] This is the truth that set me free. Jesus purchased freedom for man through His blood.[7] In Him is life and in His life is light.[8] Everything outside of Jesus is total darkness. Jesus said: *"I am the light of the world. Whoever follows me shall not walk in darkness, but have the light of life."*[9]

Jesus came to give man life: *"I have come that they may have life, ..."*[10] He proclaimed. Everything

4. Hebrews 9:26
5. John 8:32
6. John 14:6
7. Revelation 5:9
8. John 1:4
9. John 8:12
10. John 10:10

outside Jesus is only existence. There is a big difference between life and existence. A man lying in bed and dying of an incurable sickness has existence not life. A person on a sinking boat has existence, not life. The Bible says: *"He who has the Son has life; he who does not have the Son of God does not have life."*[11] To believe in Jesus is to have true life indeed.

Religion and religious deeds cannot save a person. You may say, "But I believe in God." That's not enough my friend! The Bible says: *"You believe that there is one God. You do well. Even the demons believe and tremble!"*[12] The Cross is the only way to God. The blood of Jesus is the way to forgiveness of sins. The name of Jesus is the way of salvation. *"Salvation is found in no one else, for there is no other name under heaven given to men by which we must be saved."*[13] Jesus is the only Saviour of mankind.

God has given Jesus to save the world, not to condemn it. Man's religion condemns people. Condemnation is one of the biggest problems that man faces in life. One day the religious people brought a woman whom they had caught in adultery to Jesus. They all wanted to stone the woman. They asked Jesus for His opinion. *"He that is without sin among you, throw a stone at her first,"* Jesus told them. They all left, one by one, as Jesus stooped down. He was left all alone with the woman. Then Jesus asked her,

11. 1 John 5:12
12. James 2:19
13. Acts 4:12

"*'Woman, where are those accusers of yours? Has no one condemned you?'* She said, *'No one, Lord.'* And Jesus said unto her, *'Neither do I condemn you, go and sin no more.'*"[14] Actually, Jesus was the only one who could have stoned the woman since He had never sinned. But He did not condemn her. Jesus forgave her. "For God did not send His Son into the world to condemn the world, but to save the world through Him."[15]

There is only one Way, one Truth, one Saviour and one God. Everything else is man-made and is no good.

The Bible says: *"Jesus Christ is the same yesterday and today and forever."*[16] He is the unchangeable God. Jesus does the same things that He did two thousand years ago. I have seen Him manifesting Himself in every country I have preached the gospel. I have witnessed how Jesus has opened deaf ears. I have seen the lame jump and run, the blind receive their sight and the dumb speak.[17] Some people have seen Jesus with their physical eyes during our campaigns. Others have felt His touch and have been healed and set free.

Jesus is alive and still in the business of saving people. He is the only one who can save. Jesus has authority to forgive sins. He is the one who has triumphed over Satan and sin. No other man had the power to defeat Satan except Jesus. To Jesus is given all power on earth and in heaven.[18] There is nothing

14. John 8:1-11
15. John 3:17
16. Hebrews 13:8
17. Matthew 11:5
18. Matthew 28:18

impossible for Him. He is the redeemer of mankind. Without exception He will meet with anyone who comes to Him in faith. Through faith in Him and His Word, one can see Him and His glory.[19] Jesus is standing at the door. If anyone hears His voice and opens the door, He will enter.[20]

To be saved is to open the door of the heart to Jesus and believe in His sacrifice on the Cross and believe in His resurrection.[21] By faith you can let Jesus in. By faith in His blood you can receive forgiveness for your sins. By faith in His Word you can be born again and receive the life of God. By faith in the power of Jesus' name you can be free from the bondage of Satan.[22] By faith in Jesus, the Son of God, you can please God.

"For without faith it is impossible to please God."[23]

19. John 11:40
20. Revelation 3:20
21. Romans 10:9,10
22. Acts 16:16-18
23. Hebrews 11:6

Prayer of a Sinner to
receive Jesus as Saviour

Jesus, I come to You in Your Name. Lord Jesus, receive me as You have promised in Your Word (John 6:37). Forgive my sins. I repent from them all. I now welcome You into my life. Come into my heart now, I open the door. I know You died for me and I believe that God raised You from the dead and that You are alive today. I confess You as my Lord and Saviour from now on. Thank You, Lord Jesus! Amen.

THE HARVESTERS

If you are interested in knowing more about "The Harvesters" work or in obtaining a list of video and audio cassette tapes available, please contact us:

THE HARVESTERS

Fax: +468-420727